Bad Behaviour

And Other Stories

By

Michael Higgs

This book is dedicated to

Leila

Introduction

You know how it is when you're chatting with friends at the local pub and someone says, "You should write a book about this stuff".

Well, here it is.

I finally sat down to write this autobiography after years of prompting from friends, family and complete strangers who asked me to recount various tales from my life.

A series of experiences, career choices, chance meetings, challenges and life changing circumstances were evidently far out of the ordinary, although at the time they were simply part of my daily routine.

When I began this manuscript, at the end of the first Covid lockdown, I had the intention of writing about human behaviour, and the ways in which we are similar and yet so different to the animal kingdom. Through the process of documenting 80 years… it became so much more.

This unexpected journey gave me first-hand experience of the many facets of change. From a simple, small-town 50s upbringing, through the swinging 60s and into the 70s era of free love and the many ways it translated around the world; Through the opening up of the USSR in the 80s, technological transformation during the 90s, and the shift to focus on supporting success with mindset in the early 2000s, I've been part of it all.

This was a walk through a life that turned out to be more fascinating and wondrous than anyone could have predicted – especially me!

Michael Higgs
November 2023

PART 1:

And So It Begins

Chapter One :

Early Years – Dorking

I was born in November 1943 in a nursing home on Box Hill overlooking the Surrey town of Dorking. At this time my mother, Alma Higgs, nee Lemon, had returned home to live with my widowed maternal grandfather, Alfred Lemon, while my father, Frank Higgs, a Regimental Quartermaster in the combined British/New Zealand and Canadian service under the remit of the Canadian Corps, was based down the road at nearby Headley Court. His work wasn't discussed; it turned out he was busy preparing for the D Day landings the following year.

Alma had been born in 1921. She never talked about her childhood; in fact, she didn't talk much at all. She had an older sister who had long since married and moved away and her mother, somewhat inconsiderately, died shortly after Alma's 18th birthday.

Alma had been very close to her mum and was deeply affected by her loss, but as was the way of things, there was no room for maudlin expressions of grief. Instead, an increasingly introverted and withdrawn Alma was expected to take over the running of the home, cooking and cleaning for her irascible father. This was more a duty than a joy it seems. There wasn't much in the way of affection, and lonely Alma only came out of her shell after several drinks, which ultimately is how I came into being.

Alma was average in every way. Her height and weight were very much in the median range – not too tall or short, not heavy, but not skinny either. Perhaps you could call her 'well padded' without being plump. She had coal-black hair which was smartly tied at the nape of her neck.

Initially after leaving school, Alma worked in the Scotch Wool shop in Dorking, a suitable job for young woman with a scant education. Alma had achieved a place at the local grammar school, but her father thought learning was wasted on a girl and wanted her out earning an income. She resented this injustice for the rest of her life. With the beginning of the war and the local men of fighting age either joining up or conscripted to regiments against their wishes, Alma stepped into a position previously barred to women, as Stationmaster at the tiny Boxhill railway station.

Starved of affection at home, and with limited opportunity for socialising or conversation thanks to the constraints of her solitary job, the lack of a strong maternal role model, and her domineering father, Alma's life was a disappointment to her.

One fateful night, a few sheets to the wind in the tumultuous upheaval of wartime, Alma went along to a morale-boosting dance for the troops. There she crossed paths with Frank Higgs, and, like many a young girl before and since, a few weeks later discovered her dance with a stranger had consequences which would permanently alter her future. A new generation was on the way and before it arrived, a ring and low-key wedding were required.

Frank and Alma's Wedding Day 1943

My arrival appears to have been yet another pothole in the road of Alma's unfulfilling life, preventing her from going to work where she could, for

12 hours a day at least, escape the restrictions of her father's home.

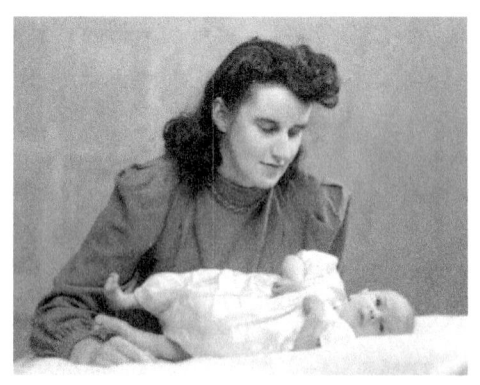

Alma with me age 3 months

With a new baby in the house, and none too pleased about Alma's inability to bring in an income, my grandfather decided he needed extra help to take care of his home and growing family responsibilities.

It seemed the obvious solution to the housekeeping issue was to recruit my father's mother Louisa Taylor. Louisa had lost her husband in 1924. He had returned from WW1 a damaged and sickly man, and Louisa, a spirited woman with a suppressed zest for life, had brought up their six children alone. She was living in desperately straightened circumstances in Tonbridge.

Louisa, known by everyone as 'Ginny' due to her taste for a certain botanical beverage, was 59 when she married Alfred Lemon. In her youth, with glossy black hair and strong features, she would have been considered handsome rather than attractive, however I recall her appearance as rather nondescript. She never stood out or drew attention. By her early 60s Louisa was somewhat dumpy, and matronly in the way grandmothers were expected to be.

Louisa was a tough old bird. Life had not been easy for her since the death of my paternal grandfather Arthur in 1924. Arthur never fully recovered from a badly timed mustard gas attack, likely deployed by the British Army, in 1918. The wind changed and blew the gas over Arthur and his fellow squaddies, leaving him physically and emotionally damaged.

Grandmother Louisa with her first husband Arthur, my paternal grandfather. My father Frank is sitting on her knee in this photo dated 1914.

Prior to her move to Tonbridge, Louisa had lived in one of the Peabody Buildings in Camberwell, taking a range of unpleasant jobs no one else wanted to do to feed her six children and keep the wolf from the door. This included assisting at the local funeral parlour, where she prepared and laid out bodies for the undertakers.

My father remembered Louisa turning unsaleable scraps from the local butcher into watery stews which were barely more than fat and water, but her kids grew up knowing right from wrong and with a roof over their heads, although anything more was an impossible dream.

Propriety being what it was, Alfred and Louisa entered a marriage of convenience to slow the wagging tongues. Thus, my maternal grandfather married my paternal grandmother creating a confusion of relatives it was difficult to unpick. However, to me it was perfectly normal, after all, didn't everyone's grandparents all live together in the same house?

Despite the decades of challenges she had endured, Louisa was a nurturing and caring individual who embraced the role of grandmother with love and affection and was resigned to her role of housekeeper. It was, after all, her position in Alf's life and this home in Dorking. She was an excellent cook and produced endless puddings and evocative aromas in her kitchen, a small, basic space with minimal utensils and, due to Alfred's limited pension and parsimony, an appallingly decrepit, but still entirely functional, gas oven and hob. Despite this she would produce the most delicious food. Her cloth-wrapped steamed puddings were a favourite and the house often filled with the scent of freshly roasted chicken.

If she wasn't cooking, Louisa would have been doing the laundry in a single tub washing machine fed by a hose. Once clean, she would lug the sopping pile of washing out to the garden to run through a heavy mangle. Women's work was hard, but she was stoic and still found time to love her little grandson.

Being in the countryside, like many of his neighbours, Alfred took full advantage of the yard, the garden of the adjoining pub and a large allotment to ensure we were virtually self-sufficient. With chickens roaming outside and pigs on the allotment with a regular batch of squealing piglets, we didn't go short of meat or eggs. Alfred wasn't the most generous of men. He would barter under duress but requests from less green-fingered locals for spare vegetables were met with a firm 'no'. However, the sickly lad who lived down the road received eggs on a regular basis. Alfred's heart might have been stony, but there was a spark of something more there.

Alfred's allotment was at least a mile and a half away. To get me out from under my mother's feet, he would take me with him, legs dangling out of the basket on the front of his heavy butcher's bike. I didn't have any 'official' purpose in the allotment garden, so I wandered around, pottered a bit and was essentially adopted by the sow as one of her many piglets.

At lunchtime, with a basket full of produce and me clinging on top, Alfred would head for the pub with me in tow. His ritual two pints prepared him his lunch and an afternoon nap. I would accompany him, then aged around three, for a half of shandy before going home to eat.

My maternal Grandfather Alfred Lemon

In the evening grandmother Louisa's other talents brought light and laughter into the home. She was artistic and somehow along the way she had learned to play the piano and had a passable singing voice. When the opportunity arose, she would be in the parlour playing quietly to herself. Evenings were a combination of pipe smoke, listening to the wireless and singing along with patriotic songs Louisa had been playing since WW1.

Living in the Surrey countryside in wartime, we had it much easier than my counterparts in the city, but even so, we didn't go unscathed. At the age of 8 months in June 1944, I was tucked in my pram, getting some air in the back garden. A doodlebug bomb hit nearby, causing glass to shatter for miles around. My mother and Louisa raced out, fearing the worst, only to find me screaming on the grass. My pram had disintegrated, but Hitler had failed to finish me off.

Me with Alma after evading Hitler

The house on Ranmore Road, despite the best efforts of the Luftwaffe, was a safe and happy haven for me in my early years, although the somewhat peculiar family set-up often caused generational and filial friction between my parents and grandparents. Nevertheless, I knew I was adored by Louisa, who was equally significant to me, and this antagonized both Alf and my mother.

My first vehicle

Alma was visibly resentful of the influence her mother-in-law had over me, and whilst appreciative of being able to work and generate a decent income (although far below that of the previous male incumbent of her job), she was probably right that Louisa had become the primary maternal figure in my young life.

Louisa's marriage to Alfred Lemon appeared devoid of love, and despite the convenience, there was always a hint of tension between them. When Alfred died in 1959, thirteen years after their marriage, 72-year-old Louisa was evicted from her home so it could be sold at the insistence of my maternal aunt.

Grandmother Louisa at Ranmore Road

It caused a bitter dispute in the family and my mother never spoke to her sister again. Louisa moved to a shabby flat in Tonbridge and I remained the apple of her eye, and the only regular visitor until her death ten years later.

Chapter Two :

Herne Bay 1946-1949

In 1946 my dad was de-mobbed from the army which was a relief all round.

Frank was tall, around the 6' mark with a toothy grin and ready smile. A short-sighted, lifelong smoker, he graduated from cigarettes to a pipe which had become his trademark.

My father, Frank Higgs

As Regimental Sergeant Major of the Pioneer Corps he had overseen supplies and logistics and was lucky to avoid court-martial after he inadvertently 'misplaced' two provisions trucks which had been parked outside the hotel where his men were billeted.

His 'error of judgement' never made it onto his curriculum vitae, and he found a job managing an ironmonger's shop on the High Street in Herne Bay, then a desolate seaside town on the north Kent coast. Wartime had left its mark and many men had not returned.

By the time Alma relocated to the town at the end of the year, she was heavily pregnant and very out of sorts.

Our first winter in Herne Bay stands out for two reasons, firstly the arrival of my younger brother Tony in January 1947, swiftly followed by one of the coldest winters in British history. The sea at Herne Bay was frozen to around 100 metres out and Louisa, who had come to take care of me while my mother was confined with her newborn in the Nursing Home, would insist on taking me out for 'air' in the subzero temperatures, which often reached -8°C.

Our clothes weren't designed for these semi-arctic conditions and there was little to excite a three-year-old, although I can remember the ring of ice around the pebbles on the beach and being walked between the high banks of drifted snow to reach home and the limited warmth of our paraffin heater.

Home was an apartment above the ironmonger's shop, part of the Mence Smith chain. The front 'public' area of the store was typical of its time with an entirely male staff in brown warehouse coats who could find the smallest, most obscure piece of hardware anyone could ask for amongst the jumble of shelves and cupboards. Paraffin and wood were the heat source for most homes and the supply was kept in the partially covered backyard. Here was a space where Health and Safety were an alien concept. A jerry can would be handed over to the storeman and taken to the yard where it would be filled to the brim. The flammable fluid would often be spilt, leaving the floor and steps slippery and dangerous while the aroma of the paraffin pervaded the entire store.

These storemen became my only real human contact. Mum was busy being a housewife and taking care of the baby, so I suppose it was easy to send me downstairs to 'help' in the shop. I became an unofficial apprentice, and to a large extent, the old boys raised me, introducing me to the way in which mechanical things worked and almost mentoring me towards what would become my first career.

In the absence of other children my age to play with, at the age of 4 my career plan was to become a storeman in a similar ironmongery shop.

Somehow along the way Mum and Dad forgot to send me to school and if I wasn't 'working' in the shop, Mum, Tony and I would go to the park or for a walk along the sea front. I was aware of other children, but never got to play with them. My entire social circle was adults and I fitted in just fine.

Mum and Dad liked to go to the local pub once a week. Tony and I would be put to bed and the two of them would disappear. It would have been normal for many working-class families; we weren't unusual or what anyone then would have described as 'neglected' although now the concept of leaving two under-fives home alone would be an open invitation for social services to get involved. I think it's fair to say, once they were ensconced in the saloon bar of one of the many seaside pubs, it would have been hard to shift them.

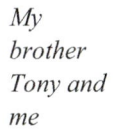

My brother Tony and me

So, as you can imagine, it came as a very nasty shock when they returned late one evening to discover the paraffin heater in our bedroom had gone out. The room had filled with oily, black soot, leaving Tony and I covered in the stuff. We were black as pitch, along with the walls, our beds, and the ceiling. Quite how we hadn't suffocated is a mystery, but my parents' pub outings ceased that night. It must have scared them beyond measure.

Alma never returned to full-time work after Tony was born, although she did use her abilities as a volunteer here and there. With the return of the nations' men from World War 2, women like Alma were once again marginalised and expected to sink back into traditional housewifely domesticity. To be fair, she ensured we were well fed with nourishing meals and prioritised caring for the men in her life and the house, using skills passed down through generations.

Alma was absolutely of her time. She wasn't remotely sporty or even that active. Despite moving to live near the coast, I don't think she ever learned to swim. She always dressed conservatively with sensible shoes and a shampoo and set. Alma, as with many women of her generation, had morphed from 'young mother' to 'matronly middle aged' in appearance without ever stopping to enjoy her 30s and 40s. Dressing stylishly was restricted to upper-middle-class ladies and beyond, and women like Alma would have been looked down on and subject to barely concealed 'no better than she should be' type comments if they stood out from the herd.

After barely surviving hysterectomy surgery in 1958, Alma and Frank's social life extended no further than the pub. She had never learned to drive, although Frank would have approved, and encouraged her to do so had she shown the slightest inclination to get behind the wheel. They stayed together through obligation and resignation. Neither wanted to become a social pariah as a result of divorce.

Alma never fully recovered from a stroke in 1974 and died in 1978. To all intents and purposes, she comes across as bland, with nothing exciting or exotic to recommend her. Looking back there was always an underlying sense of a wasted life. Alma could have been so much more had fate, her father and the system allowed.

Chapter Three:

Canterbury 1949

Dad's career took off and he was appointed a manager for the Mence Smith store in Herne Bay. This gave my parents the opportunity for an aspirational move to Canterbury and a small, rented house with a neat garden and a pleasant walk to the city centre.

Frank became a keen gardener and along with every other man on the street, grew his own vegetables and used them to avoid anything he didn't want to do or think about.

Now 5, I was a shy little boy, still a stranger to education, but that was all about to change…

School was some distance away, and a little too far for the small legs of me and a couple of other local tiddlers so, in the absence of a bus route, the local authority provided a taxi to drive us there. This service was run by a Mrs. Skam who had been using a fleet of elderly Rolls Royce's to ferry people around Canterbury forever. Thus, three little boys would arrive each morning at the Wincheap JMI school in style. Perhaps that's where my passion for large comfortable cars originated!

1953 was Coronation year, when Her Majesty Queen Elizabeth II formally received the crown of Great Britain and the Commonwealth.

Social history will tell you the event caused TV ownership to skyrocket, with families buying their first set to witness the occasion and be part of the pomp. However, on our Canterbury cul-de-sac of just sixteen houses, income was rather more modest and the investment of 60 guineas was the equivalent of spending £1400 in 2022. Television was way beyond the pockets of all but one household.

The Drons, a staunchly Baptist family, somehow scraped the money together for a brand-new TV. The small screen, perhaps ten inches across, was mounted in a floor standing cabinet and took pride of place in their parlour.

Their son Peter was my best chum, a scrawny squirty little chap with a mop of black hair and a toothy grin. In the rough and tumble world we were growing up in he was a firm friend, a lad you could rely on to get involved in whatever japes and explorations we thought up. At about this time I'd started a growth spurt and each additional inch in height elicited a combination of fascination and envy. Peter was desperate to know my secret and grow into a man.

The whole street was invited to squeeze in to view the coronation ceremony with the small room laid out as a makeshift theatre crammed full of benches and chairs cobbled together from all over the place. Peter and I bagged spots in the front row. In the end it was mostly us kids and a couple of mothers who watched the flickering images, enthralled by the magic. For the scrubbed-faced primary age kids, dressed in their Sunday best, it was not so much the ritual of the coronation, it was just that we had never seen a TV before!

After the main event, it was all very celebratory with party hats and free-flowing beer for the men, but somehow the street hadn't got the message about a full-on street party. I'm not sure whether it was even considered, there simply wasn't enough disposable income to make it happen.

Shortly afterwards Peter and the rest of the Dron family, who were a major force in the local church community, moved to the Belgian Congo to do missionary work. There was some family link to the country from the early 1900s and their decision to relocate came in the wake of an evangelical revival in the country. They went with high hopes of saving the souls of thousands of Congolese and bringing them to God.

It wasn't to be. In the early 1960s Peter Dron, still in his teens, along with his parents and younger sister Margaret were massacred in a devastating uprising, as various factions revolted against colonial rule. The news came to us much later via the local church. The shocking and unnecessary deaths of a young family whose only wish was to share their faith reverberated in our small community and the memory remains with me even now.

I frequently reflect on those lost lives, and in particular, that Peter never got a chance to grow to the height he longed for or live to his full potential. Perhaps subconsciously I wanted him to live on vicariously through me. Even now, whenever the coronation is mentioned, and particularly after the death of The Queen, my memory immediately returns to the laughing skinny boy in short trousers, sitting beside me watching the magical pictures on that tiny television.

Back in Canterbury, I was a long way behind kids of my age educationally. Starting primary school had been a struggle and I really hadn't caught up, even by the time I failed my 11+ entrance exam. The grammar school was out of the question, so I went to St Dunstan's Secondary Modern.

First day at St Dunstan's secondary modern school

Luckily, I had the opportunity to take the 13+ exam which opened the way to transferring to Canterbury Technical School for boys to specialize in engineering. Here I thrived, excelling in maths, chemistry and physics and my days of being the 'left behind lad' were a thing of the past.

The young pyromaniac

Our chemistry teacher, a young man in his very early twenties, would encourage the more enthusiastic boys to 'practise' our chemistry techniques during lunch breaks. He was particularly interested in explosive devices and four of us would brew various concoctions and then dive for cover when they ignited, leaving the dark mahogany lab bench pockmarked with embedded shards of glass which had to be cleared up before the next lesson.

My friend Albert Barber lived in an isolated house just outside Canterbury and, making use of the orchard wall, we created a makeshift lab and underground den. With scant regard to legality or safety we would liberate chemistry ingredients and take them back to his place to build guns, rockets, and other combustible contraptions.

The long summer days provided endless opportunities for experimentation and adventure of the type lads brought up in the country used to enjoy long before, and for a brief halcyon period after, 'Just William' and his outlaws cast an author's light on similar high jinks. Albert and I would head off on our bicycles with the expectation of being gone the whole day. A packed lunch of egg sandwiches in greased paper and, if we were lucky, a bottle of pop provided all the sustenance a growing boy required. Panting with exertion we'd slug up the steep hills of the High Weald and careen down them in an adrenaline-fueled rush, with zero control and a careless disregard for potential hay carts, tractors or buses which might find themselves in our path.

We believed we were invincible, assuming, with the two of us having one another's backs, we would always be safe. Of course, if there was a problem, it would be a simple matter to find a red phone box, put a coin in and press button A. If the call connected, our precious thrupenny bit would be lost, but if no one picked up the call, button B would return the money and we could come up with another solution. The phone boxes were the only means of communication out in the countryside. You never found them vandalised, they were respected by the communities for whom, thirty years before the first mobile phones, they were a lifeline and connection to the outside world.

The Technical School garnered boys from a wide area of Kent, including coastal areas close to the few remaining coal mines. There were certain areas of beach onto which coal slurry was disgorged and amongst the muck, a quick-witted lad could spot strands of cordite – the explosive used in the pits to open up new seams for mining. It didn't take long for a black-market to develop at the school – not for fags and sweets – but for cordite to use in our 'homework'.

The day we decided to combine cycling and a newly constructed home-made flare, made from a 12-inch metal cylinder filled with an orangey-brown handful of cordite strands and wadding, was sensational.

It started under clear blue sky, a balmy breeze creating waves across the barley fields, and a delicious sense of anticipation. The explosive was easily accessible, a by-product of mining operations which, happily for us, was flushed out through the tunnels onto nearby beaches following heavy rainfall, and gathered up by mud-larking lads who could sell or trade it for a profit at school.

Even the most negligent guardian angel should have had cause for concern and shouted a warning, but neither of us heard or succumbed to a moment of doubt about the wisdom of our escapade. All I will say is that it seemed like such a ripping idea to launch our newest invention one-handed from my bike.

We were in the middle of nowhere, pedaling through the idyllic fields beyond the village of Bekesbourne. The missile was balanced across my handlebars, freeing all but one finger of each hand to steer and brake as necessary. Both Albert and I were keen to assess how well it would work when launched from a moving object. As we saw it, this was science, quite literally, in motion.

I stopped briefly and set a match to the dangling string we'd rigged up as a fuse. Setting off again, steering with my left hand and holding the tube across my body with the right, it was starting to sizzle, primed and ready for action. Albert was cycling a length behind and to the side of me to monitor and observe… what could possibly go wrong?

The flame hurtled up the fuse and through the wadding faster than I imagined, perhaps the airflow had accelerated the burn time. The tube tore out of my hand and exploded right there in front of me. I saw the flash and then nothing but the azure sky as I hurtled out of the saddle, blown upwards and to starboard, landing in a crumpled heap on the grassy verge. I was floppy, still because I couldn't move, and aware of a ringing in my ears which receded into the voice of a white-faced Albert calling my name.

Astonishingly, I wasn't dead. I wasn't even scorched, although by rights I should have been badly burned across my torso and face. Instead, I lay there totally unscathed. Albie collapsed with relief beside me, and we laughed and laughed until our sides hurt.

Realising, to our disappointment, that perhaps developing mobile incendiary devices was a step too far, we decided with a casual nod to risk aversion, to confine our research to Albert's garden.

We got hold of some magnesium and made a bumper sized rocket by combining the highly volatile powder with some other bits and pieces as fuel. We'd doubtless be arrested as domestic terrorists now, but we were just two lads so fascinated by chemistry and physics, we simply extended our learning by taking our experiments home with us, not that my parents ever knew what we were getting up to. They would have locked me up!

Balanced on the top of the garden wall the rocket produced white heat and enough billowing white smoke to elect a pope. Unfortunately, the projectile, as with our many other attempts at interstellar and other explosive activity, failed to launch, but the bricks glowed white-hot, slowly subsiding into a radiant red long after we'd gone in for tea.

Albert's mother was horrified at the bomb-making going on in her garden and, with regret, we were forcibly retired from building our own small Los Alamos just off the Dover Road.

It was an unconventional childhood.

Parts of Canterbury were badly damaged during wartime bombing. It was a ten-minute walk from home from the east into the centre of the city and much of the route had been devastated. Rebuilding had started, but even so, the rubble and condemned buildings provided a precarious playground, although our parents would have disapproved. Beyond the cathedral the rest of town looked as it would have done pre-war, the small traditional streets of the historic medieval city somehow avoided the destruction.

From our perspective, the war brought an unexpected bonus. Many of the Italian prisoners of war had stayed on in Kent and opened ice cream parlours. Whilst the seaside resorts were full of them, Canterbury had only one, but it was enough. There was always somewhere to go and meet up with friends.

We were always told to avoid the two Ps – Priests and Prostitutes. My parents were horrified when they realised our favourite Italian gelateria sublet the rooms upstairs to one (or perhaps both!) of these groups.

Chapter Four:

Scouting to Success 1954

After an isolated start to life, our move to Canterbury opened the way to joining the Woodpigeon Patrol of the 8th Canterbury Boy Scouts. For a fourteen-year-old lad, this was 'the' patrol to be in and lads in the whole of east Kent looked up to the troop.

We were under the wing of a 'Rover Scout' named Ian Embrey who introduced us to life on the wild side – survival skills, stealth, foraging and self-preservation to develop our resourcefulness and make the most exciting use of the Blean Forest. I could identify edible fungi, cook a hedgehog, make bows and arrows and be safe and warm under a hedge during the wettest, gale-soaked night Kent could throw at us.

At this time Boy Scouts were almost a junior paramilitary division, or at least that's how it seemed to me. We wore green berets and second-hand army surplus kit for camping, and even excavating trenches, digging holes and on one occasion damming a farmer's field and accidentally flooding it.

Ian, with his red beret badge of office, was always at the forefront of our exploits. We would engage in 'wild games', and competition with other Scout groups and were effectively being groomed as a guerilla force. So soon after the end of WW2, we were being trained in similar techniques as the Viet Cong used against the Americans. Ian carried a woodsman's blade while the rest of us used sheath knives as part of our basic kit. No one batted an eyelid when we walked through Canterbury city centre armed to the teeth and to be honest, so soon after the end of the war with the city awash with craters, rubble, and some very unsavory characters, I think the locals were glad to have us around.

What was acceptable in the 1950s would now cost us our liberty, and yet we all found a healthy respect for weapons, the outdoor life and self-reliance, which I have no regrets about.

We could raid, capture, and trap and woe-betide any member of a rival troop who fell into one of our excavated hidden pits. As I found to my cost, it wasn't much fun to be on the receiving end of what would now be regarded as torture. My instinct for self-preservation certainly kicked in.

In an 'off the record' variation of 'take your son to work day' our patrol visited the Snowdown coal mine, the deepest colliery in the Kent coalfields. One Saturday morning we found ourselves descending almost free-fall in a cage on tethers. The lights at the bottom of the shaft raced towards us while our brains struggled to compute, creating an illusion we had stopped and were travelling upwards while the opposite was true.

Once at the bottom we were loaded onto an electric train and taken to the end of the rails where the conveyor belt to the coal seam began. This was the only access to the coal face and the mechanism was stopped to allow us to crawl along the belt through the tight, dark space almost a kilometre underground. Obeying the instruction to switch off our helmet lamps to demonstrate how dark it was at the bottom of a mine would have been terrifying, but for the reassuring presence of my companions and the knowledge I could switch the light back on.

Buckmore Park was a scout proving ground for patrols from across the southeast. The 'Wild Games' together with our camping exploits would have raised eyebrows for anyone outside the scouting organization, even then. Canny and confident at first impression, we were as feral as they came.

On one warm summer afternoon at camp, Ian made his excuses and disappeared. Leaving five young lads with nothing much to do was his first mistake. We were curious about what he was up to, so using the stalking and stealth techniques he had diligently taught us, we followed his track for a couple of miles and received a surprise education in what happens when boy meets girl in a hay-filled barn. Ian, in the throes of ecstasy, opened his eyes to find a small audience of giggling scouts observing his every move. With a roar of awkward embarrassment, his passion swiftly abated, and the girl disappeared blushing under her dress. We ran back to camp as quickly as we could, and it was never spoken of again.

Woodpigeon Scouts at jamboree

Ian was our guide, mentor, and friend. He was far from your average troop leader and had he been born ten years earlier he would probably have been one of those legendary soldiers who changed the passage of the war. Instead, he channelled his skills and talents into making us the best we could be. We were a cohesive, well-functioning group and incredibly supportive of one another – a true band of brothers.

We stuck together as a team until, a little like Peter Pan and the Lost Boys, we had to grow up and join the workforce – I'd transformed from a shy backward boy to a smart, confident self-possessed young man.

Chapter Five:

Tonbridge Transformation

Sixteen years after their marriage, my parents had saved enough to purchase their first home – a new two-bedroom bungalow in Tonbridge.

The decision to relocate was based on my father's promotion to Area Manager, and the town was more central to his region. He also had history with Tonbridge, having lived there in his early teens, and his two brothers, along with their families had never moved away.

Our spacious new home on its large plot was at the northern edge of the town. Tony and I buzzed around by bicycle, but the location meant a tedious bus ride for my mother to reach the shops. So it was altogether less convenient than the easy walk into Canterbury she had been used to.

Frank on the other hand, loved his new home in the town where he had grown up. He installed a dart board on the inside of the garage door, encouraging Tony and I to hone our skills with the arrows so we could hold our own at the pub. He loved his football and would happily spend Saturday afternoons with us at the match, either at Canterbury or Tonbridge. By the late 60s he was more likely to indulge his passion by watching the games on his small black and white TV.

Frank's social life revolved around the pub, sometimes playing darts or cards, but mostly chatting and boozing. Even once we were old enough to look after ourselves, Alma seldom went with him. I think perhaps the paraffin near-miss back in Herne Bay had permanently scarred her emotionally.

If Frank took a holiday, he might pack Alma and us boys in the car and venture southwest, often only getting as far as Eastbourne. There was a particular guest house whose friendly landlady made the pair of them welcome year after year. For Tony and me, this was less than thrilling. We hated the same old vacation and yearned for a little more excitement, but habit and minimal effort suited Frank and Alma and that's just how it was.

A holiday camp meal

By the time we reached our mid-teens, Tony and I would accompany Dad to the pub. There was a lot of smiling and joking. We shared a ludicrous and somewhat obscure sense of humour.

After a while, Dad suggested we should start calling him 'Frank' as everyone else did. We obliged and referred to him as Frank, regardless of the setting. Ironically, we frequently had to explain that 'Frank' was our dad, which rather defeated the object.

It appeared I was sprinting towards adulthood and just as every child can't wait to grow up, I was itching to try out being an adult.

Uprooted from my school friends and potential employment, my Uncle Fred suggested I look for an engineering apprenticeship at a local electro-chemical company, Wallace and Tiernan, which manufactured a range of products.

At 15 years and 8 months old I was taken on by the company, and by 16½, when my apprenticeship officially began, I was working my way around various departments whilst studying part time at technical college. Over the next five years the noise and kerfuffle of the company gave me proficiency and I enjoyed the camaraderie, practical jokes and horseplay, with my fellow apprentices Mick, George, Colin and Gerry, but there wasn't much in the way of job satisfaction.

Graduating college with my basic qualifications in the bag, I kept up my studies and was promoted within the company to join the test and research team.

Working in a brand-new facility with clients including the UK Atomic Energy Authority, Kodak and any number of airlines, my days were spent in a pristine air-locked lab running tests to calibrate and sign off high spec equipment imperative to their operations. It was a massively responsible job which meant lives were in my hands.

Focused in the calibration room

Here I was, highly qualified, experienced and gaining a great reputation, but being paid a pittance. It was time to move on, but first, let me tell you a little about the social life of a young man in mid 1960s Kent.

39

Soon after we moved to Tonbridge, I joined the swimming club. I was, at best, an average swimmer so this was less about swimming and staying fit, and more about meeting girls.

My fellow Wallace and Tiernan apprentice friends, Mick, George, Colin and Gerry lived in the north of the town and conveniently, George was the son of the landlord of a pub called the Greyhound. George was the only true engineer of the bunch, and he had a fascination for restoring cars which continued throughout his life. He could rebuild a total wreck to pristine condition. In another time he could have been James Bond's quartermaster Q, such was his attention to detail and inventiveness.

We would meet up in the back room of The Greyhound on a Friday night, with Gerry always being the first one in and the last one to buy a round. We never knew how he managed that! We were all underage, so drinks would be brought out to us, and it became our private members club. Colin's super-slick older brother Keith was self-assured with a relaxed smile and genial nature. He never needed to raise his voice the way the rest of us did to grab attention, he just held the room. Luckily for our aspirational desire to be the smartest men in town, Keith was a hairdresser, so along with the beer and good company, every other week we'd all have a short back and sides to keep us looking sharp.

The Tonbridge Boys - Mike, Keith, Gerry, George, Mick

We were a good-looking crew if I say so myself! Mick wore his strawberry blonde hair in a soft quiff which suited his wide innocent eyes. He was a little shorter than the rest of us, which made him look like the baby of the bunch. To add to his frustration, he had a very authoritarian father who restricted him from joining in with a lot of our wilder adventures. He directed his annoyance into focusing on cars and became an enthusiast, which came in handy for the rest of us when we needed transport.

Colin was a quiet, unassuming, and shyly pleasant guy. He was the one no one really noticed, especially when his gregarious big brother Keith was around.

41

Each of us was itching for our 18th birthday and this had nothing to do with being able to vote! The benefits to reaching our majority were twofold; firstly we could legally buy a drink in any pub and secondly, with testosterone-fuelled delight, we could cross the road to the church hall and join the 18+ social club.

We'd been hankering after membership since forever. The 18+ club was our Mecca, and we quickly became part of the furniture. The regular meeting night was a Wednesday, and the combination of beer and girls was intoxicating.

Now and then we'd get invited to visit a group in another town and we'd climb on a coach and head off to Maidstone or wherever for a change of scene.

The social club had brought a new pal into our circle. David, aka 'Bangers', was a third-generation butcher from a tightknit Tonbridge family. His passion for all things meat was so pronounced that on holidays and weekends away, he would make a point of visiting local butchers' shops to scrutinize and critique the windows and the quality of their mince.

It would be fair to say Bangers had been bought up in a culinarily conservative 'meat and two veg' family, so his first experience of a curry on what might be described as a 'cultural trip to Brighton' was always going to be entertaining to the rest of us. Even with the mildest dish on the menu, Bangers' taste buds had never experienced such an onslaught. Huffing and sweating, emptying pitchers full of water down his throat as he wiped ruddy cheeks drenched with tears, we laughed unashamedly at his discomfort. Heading for home, his mouth was still hanging wide open, gulping the cool sea air to tame the flames in his throat.

Bangers was an only child. As the '& Son' of the family business, his dad and uncle had included him in their sacrosanct pre-Sunday-lunch pub visit since he was a little lad. The convivial two-generation atmosphere was attractive, and before long, my own father was joining me to whet his whistle before heading home for a roast dinner.

The Tonbridge 18+ club had developed a reputation of the 'lock up your daughters' variety and there was quite a bit of mischief on group nights and on camping weekends and visits to Butlins. I guess, except for Bangers' meat obsession, we were doing exactly what subsequently happened on 18-30 holidays to Spain, we just established our notoriety ahead of the game and a little closer to home.

Between the club and the pub, our social lives were full. The only irritation was that on Sunday nights the pubs in Tonbridge, Kent, closed at 10pm whereas five miles away in Tunbridge Wells, Sussex, last orders was at 10.30pm. We would sometimes make a mad dash to Tunbridge Wells, even in winter over the hazardous snow-bound hilltop of the Bidborough Ridge, just to grab the extra pint. There was no logical explanation, just sheer joy at bucking the system.

Another frequent outing was to the Court School of Dancing in Tunbridge Wells. We'd be put through our ballroom dancing paces with classes until 9.30 and then dance on to midnight. As young men we were expected to be proficient dancers, but the company wasn't always sufficient to keep us from slipping out to the pub next door for a couple of fortifying pints to see us through to twelve am. Somehow the girls got more attractive the closer we came to the witching hour.

The Tonbridge social life was fantastic for a young man with money to spend. Even after my move to Aylesford some 15 miles away and the purchase of my first car, I would cycle back to the town for a booze-fortified night out with my friends.

As time went on, George, Keith, Bangers, Mick, Colin and Gerry, with whom I had spent much of my formative years, had worked their way through the available love-interests in the social club. The courting process meant it was something of a merry-go-round. Everyone there was engaged in a form of romantic market research to assess the merits, or otherwise, of a prospective life-partner. One of us might ditch or be ditched by a girlfriend, only for her to start seeing another member of the gang the following week.

I suppose it felt natural with our limited world view, to assume we would marry someone who had grown up in the same area with a similar background. After all, none of us really expected to move far from home. Gradually, with just one exception, each

Tonbridge boy chose a mate from the modest array of young women who attended the 18+ group.

As they fell into married life their priorities changed and within a few years my only regular contact was with George. His bride Jean shared his passion for cars and the two of them thoroughly enjoyed the car show circuit. Eventually they moved to Devon for the warmer weather and more relaxed lifestyle. I still see them occasionally.

Above: Keith and George

Below: Keith, George, Gerry, Mike, Colin

Meanwhile, back in 1966, Alma had never been enthusiastic about living in Tonbridge. She loved Canterbury, whereas even after several years, she had never settled into the way of life in Tonbridge, and the town felt quite alien to her.

She also had to contend with an underlying degree of bitterness radiating from my paternal uncles, who, quite wrongly, blamed Alma for their mother Louisa's eviction from the marital home she had shared with my late grandfather Alfred until his death. Despite their differences, Alma respected her mother-in-law and had fought for her to remain in the family home. Alma never forgave her cruel and avaricious older sister for the way Louisa had been treated, but Alma's part in trying to protect Louisa and ensure she had a home didn't suit the version of the story my offended uncles chose to believe.

Because Frank, Tony and I were content in Tonbridge we ignored our mother's disquiet. Her despondency and isolation grew, and she constantly complained of feeling unwell. With hindsight it was probably, at least partially, the impact of menopause, but none of us, including Alma, understood 'the change' or the debilitating effects on physical and emotional wellbeing. Instead, she blamed her indisposition on the area being cold and damp. If that was the case, we were oblivious to it. To the men of the family, it was a welcoming home in a wooded area, and we all loved living there. Eventually though, after a seven-year campaign of attrition, Frank gave in, sold up and they moved back to Canterbury.

Frank and Alma in a rare moment of togetherness

This time Frank was miserable. It seemed there was no way of pleasing both of them simultaneously. The significant difference in property prices between the towns meant Frank and Alma downsized into a cramped terrace house backing onto the railway. It was a significant come down for Frank and injured his self-esteem.

Tony, then aged 19, wanted to stay in Tonbridge, but was considered too young to live alone, so he moved with them and transferred to the Canterbury branch of the bank where he met and married Sandra a few years later. Canterbury was a further nail in the coffin for Frank and Alma's marriage, which had never been what might be termed a 'love match'. It entered its final phase, perhaps best described as 'mutual tolerance'.

Frank and his ubiquitous pipe

Chapter Six:

Pulp Fact

My time at the engineering company came to an end. I was now more qualified than most of my colleagues and had extensive experience in highly sophisticated projects, including being solely responsible for calibrating equipment which managed airflow through aircraft engines. Despite this, I was still regarded as an apprentice. It was time to step up.

I joined the R&D (Research and Development) department of a very large paper making company, Reed Paper Group, just outside Maidstone in Kent in 1965, aged 22. Riding around the site on a bicycle was the norm and there was a branch line linking the site to the mainline railway network to transport paper out around the country.

Luckily for me I was aligned with a senior development manager named Gerald Fayers, who immediately got me immersed in groundbreaking projects.

Thinking of the 5'8" tall bundle of physical and mental energy which comprised Gerald makes me smile to this day. He never hung around and when we had to make our way through the basement of the Reed building, a space full of pipes suspended below the ceiling, Gerald would race through, barely needing to duck. I meanwhile, at 6'2" found it impossible to keep up with him. My route would slalom and deviate to avoid the lower-level pipes, frequently knocking my head and shoulders, often unable to see where I was going and finally emerging, breathless and doubled up at the bottom of the steps to the real world.

As a learning process, my entire time at Reed was full of experimenting with novel new ideas which no one seemed to have considered repurposing for everyday use. We had the opportunity to investigate using lasers, but no one could conceive of how they might be used in papermaking – look at the world now!

Part of my role was to find ways to improve the technology which had been, more or less, unchanged for hundreds of years.

We were a team of four with our own pilot plant and a remit to be as inventive as possible. We received a regular delivery of warm papermaking pulp into a large tank which we piped around the plant and generally had a good time playing with – all in the pursuit of science.

I always went home speckled with splashes of pulp. After a few days, particularly in the summer, the fermenting pulp started to take on a unique and rather unpleasant pong, and unfortunately, we did too. Nobody ever complained, people didn't back then. It was a politer society and manual labour, farming, mining, and the associated aromas were the badge of someone who worked hard to earn a living and support their family.

Moving to Aylesford for my new job at Reed meant finding lodgings in a house with the owners and a couple of other resident houseguests. They were tolerant of the smell which lingered around me until I'd completed my ablutions on arrival home.

Between us we formed quite a tight group and as friends were always welcome, it was a very sociable environment, great for a young man newly transitioned from the parental home.

Super-friendly Monica was related to the couple who owned the house and often came round in the evenings to chat and enjoy some company while her husband was at work. She was a scorchingly beautiful brunette with a 'Sophia Loren' hourglass style. She turned heads wherever she went.

There was an instant attraction. I was utterly smitten and no one else held a candle to her in my eyes. She was gorgeous and ticked every box except one – she was married. Monica's husband worked nights and without anything to keep her at home she was bored and looking for physical distraction.

On my 23rd birthday she laid her cards, and pretty much everything else, on the table, materializing on the landing outside my bedroom in a skimpy, diaphanous nightie after a whole group of us had been out celebrating. I was young, single, and here was this beautiful woman who clearly wanted more than a cup of tea and a biscuit.

Monica insisted someone must give me a birthday kiss and that someone was to be her. We got on very well and within a couple of weeks I had fallen hard for her.

After clandestine meetings and hidden assignations, it didn't feel great being the 'other man', but lust had turned fast to love, dimmed my scruples and we soon got into the habit of spending the night together. I would arrive a few minutes after her husband left for work and leave at 6am. I spent more nights with Monica than I did in the bed I paid for.

It seemed like a foolproof situation until I woke one morning to find the path to the front door under two inches of snow. It wouldn't take a genius to notice one set of footprints leading away from the door and put two and two together, so feeling very pleased with my subterfuge, I walked backwards down the path... only to realise it now looked as if someone had gone into the house and not come out. So, mindful of Monica's reputation, I made another set of backwards prints up to the front door and then carefully inserted my feet into the tracks I'd already made back down to the road. I went to work very pleased with myself, but even so, Monica had a whole lot of questions to answer about just who had approached her front door before it even got light on that dark winter morning.

My 'secret' relationship with Monica, which it turned out was suspected by everyone except her husband, continued for years. I adored her and had she given me the nod, I would have happily made my life with her. It was tough to deal with her confusion about which of the two men in her life she wanted to be with, and that just took things round in circles, sometimes it was him, and on other occasions, me. Ultimately things cooled down after I moved away for work and our nights together became impossible. Despite that, she kept a piece of my heart with hers.

*

I was young, horny, and had no intention of being lonely for long. Even so, I was quite shy around women, especially those of my own age. It would be reasonable to say I had experience and expectations which a more innocent girl would have struggled to meet. With hindsight I was a boy vulnerable to predation, although I'd never have believed it at the time.

Frida was the archetypal Swedish blonde, but unfortunately (as she saw it) she had married in the years before free love became a thing. The swinging 60s were morphing into the hippy years of sexual liberation, and Frida believed the rest of world was having rampant sex while she was increasingly frustrated with her own, somewhat more traditional, marriage.

Looking back, I can see how hard she wanted a sexual plaything and how, for a time, I was her primary target.

Invitations for coffee at her place graduated from friendly conversation to her perching on the kitchen countertop, displaying all in an earlier version of the famous Sharon Stone pose. Clearly, she would welcome more than an offer to do the dishes.

I resisted her increasingly blatant advances, and surprisingly it wasn't too hard to do. My relationship with Monica, although secret, was very important to me. I wasn't about to mess it up with a casual fling.

Months later, after many unfulfilled kitchen displays, Frida invited me to stay over after a party. Things were cooling with Monica, and I was open to taking things a little further while Frida's husband was away on business. The other party guests noticed things were getting heated between us – Frida wasn't the type to hide her feelings and was ready to throw caution to the wind. A female friend scuppered the passion by deciding to stay over at the last minute. I was firmly consigned to the couch in order to protect Frida from making a huge mistake.

Lying there alone in the wee small hours, with my legs hanging uncomfortably over the end of the sofa, I was simultaneously frustrated and relieved. Being a toyboy had its perks, but ultimately, I wanted more, and she wasn't the girl I would choose to spend my life with.

Soon afterwards Frida and her husband moved to Beaconsfield. As it happened, I had a job interview in the area, and rang to say I would be nearby. She quickly invited me to call in before I drove home.

Despite the distance between us and my rejecting her many advances, Frida saw my visit as offering more than a little afternoon delight. She lost no time in inviting me to join her on that same uncomfortable couch while her husband was out at work.

Just as things became heated, hubby arrived home. In what felt uncomfortably like the opening of an erotic movie, Frida's husband was quick to reassure me it would be fine if I stayed… was that a twinkle in his eye?

Being old enough to know better and young enough to run, I did just that. For all Frida's charms, a ménage-a-trois in swinging Beaconsfield was not high on my list of things I wanted to do that day.

A side note on married ladies: in these more politically correct days, my behaviour, or that of my companions may be frowned upon by anyone who wasn't young, free, and periodically single from the late 1960s to the mid-1980s. Indeed, reading this book you might have gained the impression the married women I became involved with were harlots, or "no better than they should be" as my mother might have said.

This does them a disservice. My paramours were normal, friendly, sociable human beings. There was nothing cheap about them, or indeed in our relationships. We went in with our eyes open, and I regret nothing.

What led each to take a decision to look beyond their marriage was their healthy appetite for sex and a desire for connection. For Monica, Justine, and Frida their physical, and often their emotional needs too, were not being met by their husbands. Although the concept of 'free love' might have received a lot of press coverage and been welcomed with open arms by many Kodak employees, (and apparently in suburban homes with pampas grass!), such openness in relationships wasn't the norm by any stretch of the imagination.

The women who embarked on affairs with me at their own instigation were adventurous and wanted to be liberated in a time when divorce was still regarded as shameful. Leaving a marriage, even one which was loveless or abusive, potentially left a woman and her children destitute. Men held the balance of power financially as well as morally in the eyes of society, regardless of their own peccadillos.

*

Towards the end of my time at the Reed Paper Group the company was rapidly moving away from ancient practices to having computer panels everywhere. What seems obvious now, at a time when almost anything can be controlled by a mobile phone, would have been inconceivable back then. The big plan was to create the first computer-controlled paper-making machine anywhere in the world. The sheer scale of the computer hardware was huge, but nevertheless we were well on track to achieve our goal to transform the process when everything fell apart due to cheap imports from the Far East.

The industry was having a tough time and redundancies were in the air. As the youngest, and with my single status taken into consideration, I flew to the top of the list.

Although the company were motivated to find me new employment and the personnel department tried hard, the options locally were low-level technical work. There was nothing which remotely compared to what I had been doing with technology and innovation and to put it bluntly, the pay was considerably worse.

I was cut loose with no idea what would happen next.

PART II

Moving Onwards and Upwards

Chapter Seven:

Starting Again

Realising I had to change direction as my redundancy was looming, I spoke to people who might have some ideas for me - I was still quite young, naïve, and very much a 'lad' looking for guidance and direction from my elders.

A friend suggested the Daily Telegraph on a Tuesday. I picked up a copy, probably the first time I had read it, and trawled through the advertisements. There was a position at Kodak which seemed a close match to what I had been doing. They were looking for engineers to help implement and run a state-of-the-art film making facility. I applied and after a lengthy and remarkably thorough interview process, I was offered a job which I gratefully accepted.

The complex was still being built in Harrow and it was huge. From the outside it resembled a large hotel, although that was just the part I could see. It was quite the landmark in a country still marked by the damage of the war.

My only reservation was that it was on the wrong side of the Thames for me. I'd grown up in semi-rural Kent, lovely countryside on hand and close to the sea.

Anything north of the Thames was alien, it might have well as been another planet. This was a time when it was unusual to leave the town you grew up in and many of my friends thought they would never see me again. Funnily enough, I still see them now, over 50 years later!

So, I relocated to Middlesex and the sprawl west of London to begin my career at Kodak in August 1968. I won't dwell on the technical stuff, you'll probably nod off if I do, but suffice to say my life gradually changed over the next few years in a way I could never have conceived.

Chapter Eight :

A Company Town and Ethos

My time at Kodak led me into an all-encompassing relationship with a company which dominated the lives of its employees to such a degree that many of my colleagues lived fully through the company, with couples meeting, marrying, and socializing on site with no need to look beyond the boundaries of the Kodak village.

Security was extremely tight. The restricted part of the site was strictly controlled and only accessible by a swipe card pass (very new technology at the time). Whilst in 21st century Britain kids now access school via a magnetic pass, this high-tech degree of caution was unheard of in 1968.

The site was an oasis of light in Harrow, having originally been opened in 1890. By the 1960s it had expanded to cover 55 acres of farmland on the edge of London. Some of the buildings, known as Track 1,2,3 and 4 used equipment from the early part of the century – antique to my eyes. Track 5 however was bang up to date and that's where I worked in the early part of my time at the company.

Track 5 was 50 metres long, 20 metres wide and 5 stories high. The first four floors were all about making film and contained a huge control room accessed through 'light locks'. Outside this control room were 'light locks' where the light got progressively dimmer towards the manufacturing area where the remaining space was filled with complex heavy machinery and maintained in darkness. This was where film was coated in stages, and any light would have damaged the process. The entire building was a cathedral to film assembly.

However, the complex machinery, a little like painting the Forth Bridge, had to be constantly monitored and maintained. This meant donning night vision goggles and wriggling up to 20 metres in pitch dark crawl space through tight noisy gaps between clanking, spinning, and grinding machinery. I would be on my own, with no real consideration for Health and Safety, to use a meter on every piece of kit which needed to be reviewed and checked to reassure us it was working efficiently. Any problem with the equipment would mean it would have to be stopped and may take hours to do the equivalent of re-booting the technology then cleaning up the inevitable spills of unpleasant coating emulsion.

Kodak was ahead of the game in so many ways, and sustainability was one of them. All the sludge created by the film making process was collected in tanks and recycled to remove the silver and other products for resale rather than dispose of the spoil down the drain.

The company had created a 24/7 mini city which was almost self-sufficient. Few businesses could boast of their own power station – plus cooling towers which became an iconic landmark in Harrow. Having power meant Kodak continued to run 24/7 even during the three-day week in 1974, when other industries in the UK were forced to limit working hours due to power cuts and industrial action dictated by unions and strikes.

Staff at Kodak had no interest in striking. With exceptionally high pay rates, significant annual bonuses and great benefits, the on-site union representatives had very little to do. Kodak recognised it was worth keeping staff happy in order to maintain production, so that's what they did. The knock-on effect was felt by the town of Harrow and the surrounding area with car dealerships taking the bulk of their annual profits in the weeks after the March bonus distribution.

A site with so much flammable material needed swift fire support and Kodak maintained a full fire station with engine, turntable ladder, crane, and fireman's pole. If there happened to be a fire emergency in the local area, it wasn't unusual for the Kodak team to go out in support of the civilian firefighters. Even with the fire department, all Kodak staff were rigorously trained in fire safety to mitigate risk. Aside from anything else, Kodak were self-insuring, so any fire would have been catastrophic both practically and financially.

Several massive car parks catered for the 7000 strong staff, many of whom worked on shift, and where their job was positioned in the company hierarchy determined the location of their parking space. Illness and vaccinations were managed by the medical centre. I could go there in the middle of the night and receive immediate care from a nurse. This facility did all my pre-travel vaccinations and ensured I stayed well without having to take time out from work to visit my local GP.

Kodak's ethos was to be at the centre of its workers' lives and for many their focus completely revolved around the site.

Just outside the secure area was the community facility including a large bar, recreation area, 200-seat theatre/cinema, and dining areas. On another part of the site were football and rugby pitches, squash, and tennis courts and even a shooting range for rifles and handguns. Between the various leagues, clubs, groups and societies, this utopia provided almost everything an employee might need or want. For many employees their work and social life was completely controlled by the company - they only went home to sleep.

From the 50s through to the 80s it wasn't unusual for a large business to have a staff restaurant on site. Like everything else about Harrow, Kodak did it on a bigger scale with separate subsidised dining halls for the blue collar staff (factory floor) and white collar staff (office based) seating 300 people at a time. Dining could be quite territorial and beware the junior member of staff who inadvertently sat in the wrong seat! Executives enjoyed an a la carte dining room with crisp linen and white tablecloths, which was available for managers and senior staff only when a particular pay grade was reached. The executive 'lunch club' could be booked for VIP guests to the site.

The dining areas in the manufacturing buildings worked 24/7 to cover the shift patterns and with 24-hour working I could sit down to a roast dinner at 2am if I chose to do so.

For all the 'community' ethos, Kodak was a very status conscious environment, and the majority of staff embraced the concept of everything being pre-ordained based on your position within the company. The buildings had separate lavatories for managers to prevent them from having to mix with more lowly staff. The key to the executive w.c. was very much a sign that you had made it to the higher echelons of Kodak society.

I never really gave the situation much thought whist I ascended the hierarchy at Kodak. Looking back, I wonder whether the self-reliance and paternalistic control of Kodak was part of the American 'company town' philosophy or it was just of its time. Either way, I can't imagine many companies would be able to have such an impact on the lifestyle of their staff these days.

Chapter Nine :

Kodak Sailing Club

Part of the Kodak sports package was a sailing club with our own yacht moored in the marina at Lymington on the Hampshire coast.

I wanted to learn how to sail and take advantage of the new experience, so despite being a complete novice, and alongside a colleague, I took the opportunity to join a sailing party for a few days. However, I questioned my judgment when, on arriving at the yacht, I found the skipper waiting for me.

Despite his nondescript appearance, 45-year-old Ralph was renowned for being a dominating and strict man and was widely disliked in his role as a Kodak shift supervisor in my department. The thought of spending a few days trapped at sea with him, despite being his equal in terms of the company hierarchy, left me somewhat wary. The skipper was the captain of our ship – he was in charge!

My concerns turned out to be completely unjustified. It transpired there was a different side to Ralph, far from the demanding and critical 'work persona', which his team saw. I was lucky to be a beneficiary of the 'real man'. As a qualified skipper he could take the yacht out and was a patient, friendly instructor who got the best out of everyone.

The plan was to sail around the Solent and then cross to the French coast and on to the Channel Islands.

After the first day of initial training, we set off on a particularly stormy night, sailing towards France in the cold, wet darkness.

The routine was to have one person at the helm whilst the two others slept in four-hour shifts. After just a few hours on board, I was in charge for the midnight to 4am stint, sailing into the wind and constantly buffeted by spray and rain.

It was miserable. Huge container ships were doing around 20 knots all around us whilst the yacht was barely managing 5 knots and attempting to cross in front of them against the high waves and wild sea. Despite the beacon and radar, we were pretty much invisible.

Bobbing from side to side, soaked through, unable to see through the salt and spray, it was almost impossible to steer any reasonable course, let alone avoid anything big and nasty. In the end I had no option other than to get under cover and hope they would see us on radar from far enough away to avoid a Titanic moment.

Somehow, despite my lack of experience and ability, we made it unscathed and once the storm had passed, we spent the next few days with Ralph teaching us more about sailing and visiting the islands.

Moored in the small harbour at Alderney we went ashore for a beautifully cooked evening meal at a local pub. After a few drinks the harbour tender returned us to the yacht where, rather than making a gazelle-like leap onto the deck, I somehow managed to fall into the sea. I'd like to think it was the slippery ropes which caused my dunking rather than any overindulgence on the local beer, but I'm not sure the harbour master would agree.

I'll never know if Ralph deliberately chose a strict work persona because he felt it was the only way to progress in the company. Whoever he really was, I was proud to sail with him.

Chapter Ten :

Theatre and Other Extra-Curricular Activities

Some while after joining the company I was encouraged to join the Kodak Theatre Group. I was working long shifts and not doing very much socially, so Gill, an office co-worker with an eye for a good-looking lad suggested it would be a change of scene.

Each year the group rehearsed and staged three shows, a play in the spring, a musical during autumn and the Christmas pantomime. The same stalwarts were in everything, year after year, and kept the theatre running.

A group of younger employees were drawn to the theatre group. Most were in long term relationships, often with their other halves working for Kodak too. Some used the opportunity to indulge in illicit affairs with other members of the cast. They were looking for fun, and the theatre 'luvvies' were happy to provide it or at least provide a safe haven for it to happen. The group was a hotbed of affairs and intrigues.

The younger women would literally spray-scent their male conquests, joining them in the dressing room to 'do their makeup'. Other theatre members just turned a blind eye to what was going on; it was just part of the am-dram scene.

I turned up for my first rehearsal with Gill and was introduced to the cast. One girl stood out, petite, slim, well groomed, with an infectious, conspiratorial laugh. Justine was a devastatingly attractive woman, blonde hair and a convent education. She was 21, I was 23 and darn it, she was married.

Nevertheless, Gill confided to me later that evening, Justine had told her she was "going to have him".

So inevitably we started seeing one another. By the hot summer of 1976 we were involved in a steamy affair.

We'd meet up in Berkhamsted, and local villages close to the town, just far enough away from her husband to be unnoticed. Lunchtime assignations were a regular thrill with her in a short skirt and no knickers. She was adventurous. Women's autonomy was in full force, thanks to the pill, and the concept of free love was fairly routine in the circles I moved in.

Understandably, her marriage was on the rocks. She'd married on the rebound anyway. Her husband was a nice guy, quiet, sensible, and hard working. He had no idea what was going on.

Subsequently I discovered I wasn't the only one Justine was involved with. She had another chap on the go simultaneously and reached the stage of trying to pimp me out to her sex-starved friends. I declined that offer and moved on from our relationship.

She was pure predatory female. Justine had been abandoned by someone she was passionately in love with, married the first guy who asked her, and was determined from then on to take charge of her physicality and her attitude to life and sex was "Sod it, I'm just going to enjoy myself."

Shortly after I joined the theatre group, I had a small part in the pantomime, Aladdin. In a complete absence of colour-blind casting, I wore brown make up on my face, torso, and lower legs to complement my bolero and pantaloon costume. I couldn't quite believe I was singing and dancing, it was something I never expected to do, but I loved the joyous relationship with the audience.

The only drawback was that the make-up was such a faff to remove. I tended to leave it there until the following morning and shower off just before work.

Meanwhile, back in the wings, the inter-cast romances were in full flow. You were either being groped, groping, or averting your eyes at some risqué behaviour. The women, contrary to many assumptions these days, were actively pursuing any reasonably attractive man, and even the most strait-laced chap was a target. Anyone who was single was an easy option for their lusty advances.

At the time, it just seemed like harmless fun. It appeared everyone was doing it, although that probably wasn't actually true. For us it was just 'The 70s'.

That spring I was cast in a major acting role in a play 'Goodnight Mrs Puffin'. I found a new passion, and despite some nerves, once I stepped onto the stage I was completely caught in the moment.

During this period, I was sharing a house with a guy named Dave. He was living in a large four bed place, previously his family home, although his wife and kids had left him.

Dave also worked at Kodak, and he wasn't the most popular guy in town. However, being available put him in the 'eligible for anything' category. He was a regular visitor to sex clubs and the hot spots of Thailand, and this made him an exciting conquest for the women we knew, both at work and in a local pub where we took shifts to meet new friends.

There was a competitive edge between us. As a full-on alpha male, he always believed his girlfriends were of a higher calibre than the women I was seeing.

After a while I got bored with the atmosphere, which could be uncomfortable. By the time we reached the stage of tolerating one another I knew it was time to leave. Coincidentally, my Thursday night over -30s club brought a new landlady into my life. Carrie.

Carrie was a picture-perfect 1970s woman, she hid her intense hazel eyes behind enormous sunglasses and with her slim, toned body, perfect teeth and flicked soft caramel Charlie's Angel's hairstyle she stood out wherever she went. She loved to dance, a true disco queen, always ready to do the Hustle and give Gloria Gaynor a run for her money.

As was the way of things, the landlady/tenant arrangement morphed into something more. We became a striking couple, and I took pride in having her on my arm when out on the town. She was popular with my brother and his new wife too. We cruised through a couple of years, sharing the moment Elvis died on that hot summer night in August 1977. We were flirting with the idea of making things more permanent, but change was in the air and maybe the stars didn't align in the same way anymore.

Taking my cue from Paul Simon, I selected one of the 50 ways to leave your lover and we separated without regret or ever looking back.

Chapter Eleven :

Doris Stokes

Google describes Doris Stokes thus:

"Doris Stokes was a celebrated medium who confounded skeptics by the uncanny accuracy of her readings."

Early in my relationship with Carrie, while the glow was still white hot, but we knew almost nothing about one another, Carrie's friend Peggy was enjoying new love with a chap who also happened to be named Mike.

Peggy was keen to find out if Mike was a good long-term bet so with Doris Stokes in town, she and Carrie went off for a consultation.

On their return they were dismissive of the information Peggy had received – it didn't seem to fit her situation at all, and poor old Doris's reputation was ruined as far as Peggy and Carrie were concerned.

I sat there listening, becoming increasingly intrigued and wide eyed as fact after fact was precise and pertinent to me. It was really solid and incontrovertible information – places I had lived, family names and situations, even my work history.

The thing is, neither Carrie nor Peggy knew any of this – they barely knew more than my name at that point in time. It felt to me as though Doris was tuning into the energy of the wrong man!

Apparently, Doris had told the girls that she "really wanted to meet this man because he has a very strong aura, and you must get him to come to see me."

I'm sure this celebrated medium was genuinely expressing her view rather than pitching for business. She didn't need extra clients; she was internationally famous and making huge amounts of money from live shows and working with celebrities. While I was curious, I chose not to go and see her. Why? With hindsight I think I was a bit scared of what else she would reveal.

Sorry Doris – not coming to see you was something I still regret!

Chapter Twelve :

Changing Direction

I was an engineer, I liked research and development, but at the heart of everything was my love of engineering. Somehow though, along the way, I started to train others in the implementation of the specialist equipment and teaching other much more experienced operators how to use the brand-new technology Kodak was bringing in.

I found I was really enjoying it. Many of the old guard were used to antiquated machines and struggled to grasp the new technology, but it was a doddle for me to retrain them. Within a couple of years, I was acknowledged for my ability to share these new skills in a way which worked for everyone. Transferring to the training department was a natural progression, but the thing was, once you joined the training team, nothing was off the table. We were teaching just about any subject which was fashionable at the time. I'd learn it one week and be teaching it the next! As my knowledge increased my horizons expanded. Now I was teaching throughout the UK… I had finally overcome my fear of travelling North!

It turned out Kodak had even bigger plans for me. This was a company which really was ahead of its time in terms of developing staff and creating an accomplished workforce which thrived on expertise.

Soon afterwards I was asked to run a programme at a Kodak training facility in Holland. The students were from all over Western Europe and their command of English was variable – but it is fair to say their English was infinitely better than my command of any of their languages! I quickly learned to modify the words I used and the speed at which I spoke. The flipchart became my best friend, and I would leap around the classroom like an enthusiastic gazelle to illustrate my point.

The great thing was the students enjoyed it as much as I did. I continued to teach around the world – somehow Kodak had provided an opportunity for travel that small-town boy from Kent could never have imagined.

Chapter Thirteen :

Julia

I used to go to a dance club in Greenford, West London, for the Over 30s night on a Wednesday. There were any number of girls there – married and single – enjoying a midweek interlude. It was a fantastic place to meet people away from the confines of the Kodak bubble.

Julia was a bombshell and could have been a screen-siren. She was a desirable Claudia Cardinale lookalike. Voluptuous, Italianate with a raven bouffant up-do and mesmerizing chocolate eyes. She was always beautifully dressed and arrived at the club each week with her sister. I'm sure the sister's husband thought his wife was enjoying chaperoned entertainment – the reverse was true! Julia's sister was busy with other dancers, and not always on the dance floor.

Julia had been living in Zambia until her divorce and had returned to London relatively recently. She was very family-oriented and had bought a house to settle down with her teenage sons and be close to other members of her family. She spent a lot of time visiting them, and they were a commanding part of her life.

If Julia's childhood had been catholic, she was spending her adult years making up for lost time. Justifiably proud of her body, Julia had professional topless photographs taken and they were hung resplendent over the mantelpiece, proudly displaying her assets to her sons, their friends and anyone else who visited her home. Quite what her doting parents thought of her ample attributes being there for all to see I have no idea, but it certainly wasn't kept secret.

Julia loved to portray herself as confident, fashionable, and sexy, but underneath the bravado she was fundamentally introverted and said it was an illusion. Her ex-husband would never recognize the woman other people perceived she had become.

I was keen and asked her out but initially she messed me around quite a lot. It only made me want her more.

I was by now in my late thirties and open to the idea of finding 'the one'. Julia was exciting, and my feelings grew quickly. She was lovely inside and out, something you didn't experience very often. When she finally agreed to start seeing me, I found she was also physically adventurous and incredibly passionate – a rare combination indeed. It was quite a novelty to be dating someone who was available rather than sneaking around behind a husband's back.

But it seemed I was still a 'friend with benefits' rather than a serious contender for her heart. Yes, we were intimate, going out as a couple and spending weekends together, but I didn't get the impression I was as significant to her has she was to me.

Frolicking on her sofa one evening we had reached the point of no return when the door opened and one of her sons wandered through the room, said 'hello' and went on into the kitchen completely unperturbed. I couldn't help wondering whether this wasn't the first time he'd seen his mother in flagrante.

We were together a couple of years, revelling in the security of a loving relationship. We were open to the idea of experimenting with the pleasures of swinging or meeting other couples for sex and on one occasion travelled to a pub in Berkhamsted (it is remarkable how often the town features!) to meet up with a couple for some fun.

Julia, being dazzlingly attractive was quite the enticement, but on this occasion, we were frustrated in our intention. They couldn't get away fast enough. It seemed they would only consider frolicking with a married couple – it was safer that way and blatantly obvious from the way Julia and I behaved that we hadn't fallen into the marital rut.

But all good things have their time.

Gradually I became more reluctant to see Julia and my travelling for work was a good excuse to put some distance between us. Our dates continued, but more by habit on my part.

As is the way with these things, as I pulled back emotionally, she decided I was the man for her and declared her wish to be together permanently. Her timing was badly out. Just a couple of months earlier I would have taken her shopping for a ring and waltzed her up the aisle, but she'd left it too late. It wasn't the whole 'treat them mean, keep them keen' thing, I'd just lost interest in her treating my affection so casually.

As chance would have it, fate intervened one sticky summer night, and when a couple of days later I ended it with Julia she was desperately upset.

Would it have worked out? Could it have worked out? I'll never know. A decade later a book called 'The Rules' was published. The premise was that women should keep men at a distance, be unavailable and keep their suitors waiting. By doing so the men would fall at their feet in complete devotion. Reading the reviews, it seemed Julia had followed those Rules to the letter.

The sad thing was, I never got the memo!

Chapter Fourteen :

Leila

For a very long time I led a bachelor life, having a few medium-term relationships lasting a year or two, Julia being the most recent, and until our time together it suited me not to be overly tied to one person. The people I was seeing socially, all of whom grew up in the 60s/70s, mostly felt the same way.

In June 1985 I was invited to a party at the Bricket Wood Cricket Club by a pal. I'd only just flown into England and picked up the answer-phone message purely by chance, but still, it was something to do after a long time out of the country.

Standing at the bar were two women; a well-nourished blonde and an immensely attractive, elegant, slight girl with flaxen hair bubbling around her shoulders, who could only have been of Scandinavian extraction.

Both seemed very keen to talk to me and my friend was definitely playing second fiddle.

For me there was no contest. I asked the Abba-esque girl to dance. She was something else and I was smitten. Without realizing who I was looking for to share my life with, Leila discoed her way in and never left.

Leila grew up in small rural village in the Lemi municipality in southern Finland made famous by the composer Sibelius. She was a middle child with an older sister and younger brother. Although the family was regarded as poor, they were one of very few in the area to own a car.

I never knew her father's name, he had died in 1960 having never fully recovered from a grenade injury sustained in the Winter War against Russia. After his death, Leila's mother Hillke was destitute and totally reliant on support from relatives. Leila hated moving from one farmhouse to another as they exhausted the welcome of her increasingly inhospitable uncles and aunts, ultimately moving to Helsinki where Hillke found work. It was no wonder the bright lights of Europe were so alluring.

Age 20, Leila travelled to England with a friend and got a job in a care home in Bishop's Avenue, a very expensive part of London close to Regents Park. Soon afterwards, keen to reinforce her residency in the UK, she met and married a guy named Alan and settled in Hatfield.

We rapidly became close and within weeks I'd moved in. Leila already had a daughter, Sarah, who was eight at the time and we soon settled in to playing happy families.

Before I met Leila, I had been seriously considering leaving Kodak and going to live in Spain. My plan was to find a place I liked and initially use it for holidays before potentially relocating permanently when the perfect time arose. I imagined the sunny expat lifestyle would really suit me and there wasn't anything tying me to the UK.

At that point everyone seemed to be buying Timeshare property and there were some amazing options to choose from, but I knew being constricted to certain weeks each year wouldn't suit me or my nomadic career. I wanted my own space, furniture and possessions in situ, and the flexibility to pick up my passport and jump on a plane without having to plan or pack.

The town I found my way to was Calpe on the Costa Blanca, an attractive and relatively small place with a traditional fishing-harbour and active community.

I bought a 6th floor town-centre apartment, slap bang in the middle of things, overlooking a private swimming pool and just 200 metres from the beach. Everything was within easy walking distance, and I could completely switch off from the pressure of work to indulge in delectable food and wines while getting to know the locals and making new friends.

After Leila came on the scene several months later, with a sunny destination accessible to her at the drop of a hat, we'd visit frequently to enjoy quality time together as a family.

Leila loved to tan on a lounger positioned far enough from the pool to avoid the distraction of splashing kids, and dive-bombing squeals. She'd bake gently, nose in a book, lost in a chick-lit world of romance, friendships, and unlikely inheritances. The place was the perfect antidote to the restrictions of her office-based job, although annoyingly she wasn't willing to release the controlling part of her nature and was absolutely rigid about the 'correct' time for lunch. Beware a hungry daughter or boyfriend asking to eat before 2pm! Sarah and I did sometimes win the battle with a tag-team combination of beseeching looks, whining, extortion, or a well-placed 'hangry' comment. More often than not though, we prowled impatiently, stomachs growling, waiting for the minutes to tick by just willing Leila to glance at her watch, set the book down, and come to join us.

While Leila was so deeply absorbed, Sarah and I would lark about in the pool for hours, swimming and sploshing, laughing raucously as we spritzed passing staff, and making the most of the sunshine. Sometimes we'd head to the beach or watch the fishermen bringing in the catch in the harbour. It was a blissful way to wind down and share a magical life together.

In the evenings, Leila and I could indulge in the freshest seafood. We grew to know the resident expats who become more than acquaintances and looked forward to seeing us. As she grew up, Sarah was able to bring along friends to keep her company, so we could all relax and enjoy the holiday without Sarah being obliged to tag along with us if it didn't suit her.

Leila and I were happy and deeply in love. The fly in the ointment was that although she was separated, Leila hadn't yet been divorced from her husband and Sarah, who was the archetypal 'daddy's girl' adored her dad, and increasingly resented Leila and me. She really did not want me as a permanent fixture in her life.

The situation was exacerbated by the close proximity of Leila's ex, who lived nearby. Alan was a big, athletic guy. Good looking, taller than me and with a crop of fair hair, he definitely stood out in a crowd. He worked in a car repair shop and was hands on and very practical. Alan and Leila had got together almost as soon as she arrived in the UK and after 13 years of marriage, Leila appreciated his DIY prowess. One of her few bugbears as far as I was concerned, was my complete disinterest in anything which involved a toolbox. Our rare disagreements usually began with the words "Alan would have fixed that".

Sarah was protective of her father. Still young, she didn't understand that Leila had invested in a 'rental' flat with the specific intention of asking Alan to move into it as a first step to ending their marriage, something which happened long before I came on the scene.

Alan wasn't enthralled by the situation either. It didn't help that we were living in his old marital home, and he'd turn up with a proprietary attitude, park his car on the drive and like any wounded animal, behave antagonistically towards the upstart who had replaced him. After almost coming to blows on a couple of occasions, he pushed too far. For the first and last time I stood up to him. No punches were thrown, and no harm done, but Alan knew he'd met his match.

After a short time managing the uncomfortable situation with Alan, we sold our respective houses and bought a larger place together. The relocation took us slightly further away from Leila's married life and gave us a fresh start in a home of our own.

This really was getting serious!

Chapter Fifteen :

A Russian Incursion

Fourteen months after we met, Leila felt sufficiently confident in our relationship to introduce me to her Finnish relatives. Arranging a series of stays with relations she had hardly seen since moving to the UK, we travelled to Finland with Sarah.

This was a time when entrepreneurial Finns would take a trip into the USSR on a semi-regular basis. Although ostensibly they crossed the border as tourists, there was an undercurrent of smuggling as well as the desire to travel. Staying with some of Leila's relatives and looking for something different to do, four adults and a little girl decided to drive to Leningrad in Russia. The city has now returned to its original name, 'St Petersberg' but then back in 1986 it was firmly in the grip of communism.

We would need visas, and it wasn't at all certain we would get them. After several visits to the travel shop the documentation was provided and allocated to our vehicle.

The paperwork recorded the combination of Finnish and British passengers, something guaranteed to cause consternation for the border guards when we reached Vyborg to be met by several severe Russian guards. These guys looked and acted as though they'd just stepped out of a spy movie and when they demanded our papers with an unnecessary degree of force, we wondered whether we might have slipped into one.

There was a much younger Russian man with an enthusiastic cocker spaniel, a sniffer dog ready to find whatever contraband we might be carrying with us. The handler, uniquely, was relaxed. While the guards took forever over our papers, the dog and its owner turned the car inside out. Nothing, but nothing, untoward was getting into Russia that day.

Until this point all conversation had been in Finnish and Russian. My Finnish companions, aware of the long drive ahead of us, wanted to be on our way and said they were fed up with the delay. I was more sanguine – reminding them in English that we knew the border guards would be thorough and it was a nice day to be standing in the sunshine.

The dog handler stood nonchalantly at my elbow and said in excellent English "Yes, it is a nice day isn't it." A smiling Bond villain in disguise.

As we drove away the guards saluted the dog handler dutifully, showing their respect to a senior officer from a very different part of the Russian armed services.

Across 20 miles of Russian designated no-man's-land we passed huge car parks, vast swathes of tarmac and concrete housing not cars, but massed tanks and artillery pieces. Stretching as far as the eye could see the gun barrels pointed to the sky in a silent macabre salute to some Soviet war god.

Even without signage, we knew the area on either side of the road was heavily mined so pulling over or stopping to get a better view was not an option. Travellers knew you didn't wander onto the scrubland and woe betide anyone who stood on a bare sandy patch amongst the roadside gorse.

When we arrived at the immigration hall, a dark, forbidding building marking the end of no-mans-land, a young Russian woman scurried towards us having instantly recognised me from the visa photos which would have been forwarded to her. She informed me breathlessly that she was to be my interpreter. It must have been a novelty to use her English – no other Brits were expected that day, or on any other. An Englishman arriving by car was highly unusual, and coming in via Finland was unheard of. We were very closely watched.

We finally cleared the bureaucracy of entry into the USSR and made our way out onto the long road to Leningrad, still several hours away. Cars were few and far between and we had the road pretty much to ourselves – well just us and the secret service people designated to follow us throughout our time in the country.

It wasn't hard to spot them, especially when they lost us after we stopped for a comfort break, and they somehow drove past. Minutes later their car came screeching into the layby, evidently more relieved to have found us than we had been to empty our bladders. We waved and smiled as we drove off.

If those guys had actually lost us, their jobs and probably much more would have been on the line. Our presence in the USSR was of very great interest to some dangerous people and our followers were just small, dispensable cogs in a much bigger machine.

Every village we drove through had a command post in the centre and as we passed each one, the guard would pick up a telephone to report our presence. With little traffic and Finnish plates, we had gained an uncomfortable degree of celebrity.

But it wasn't just the secret service watching our every move; mobile currency traders would overtake us gesturing they would exchange dollars for hard currency at three times the official rate. Three fingers which would be upgraded to four if we waved them away. My Finnish companions steadfastly avoided the temptation – the police used this as a sting tactic for foreigners looking for the best deal.

When we finally reached Leningrad, we were constantly under surveillance. The resources which went into this were immense. Our hotel rooms were carefully checked each time we went out – you can always tell when your possessions have been rifled and two days in it was par for the course. To the Russians I was not a tourist, they believed I was there for reasons of espionage and were determined to find out why this Englishman was travelling with a group of Finns and a child. Even without cameras and ANPR and with their men reliant on basic technology and shoe leather, we had followers haunting us in battered cars and on foot for the entire duration of our stay.

Our tails turned out to be an unexpected bonus when one of them noticed a bag-snatcher closing in on us. The spook made up the distance unseen and took down our assailant, leaving him winded on the pavement. All of us, including our minder, quietly returned to our walk while the would-be thief lay thwarted on the cobbles.

We made a visit to the Winter Palace. I had expected to be wowed by the juxtaposition of impressive buildings in comparison to the chill utilitarian blocks which were such a dominant feature of the USSR. In the 1980s the façade was in a pretty poor state of repair and 60 years of communist rule had left the baroque monument to imperialist Russia looking more like a disheveled boarding school than the exquisite palace of the history books. Knowing a little of its history and in my mind's eye having imagined the centre of absolute power for Catherine the Great and the Romanovs having retained at least a little of the essence of the Tsars; the jewel of St Petersberg had been punished by the Reds and was a sad disappointment to us all.

History is re-written by those who come afterwards, and it is interesting now to see the apparent return of absolute power under President Vladimir Putin being reinforced by the refurbishment of the Winter Palace and indeed the beautiful architecture of modern-day St Petersberg as a destination for Western tourists.

But I digress. The Soviet Union as it still was on that first visit, was a place of queues and empty shelves. I could not conceive of how underprivileged the population were, knowing the country was a global superpower at the forefront of the arms race and with massive spending power. Any visit to a supermarket, even for something as simple as bread, was a lengthy affair; queue outside, take a ticket, queue some more and hope the store had what you wanted when you finally made it in. It was so protracted we decided to leave the first store and look for another much to the astonishment of the stoic Russians behind us who were waiting in the hope of bananas. The next store had nothing on the shelves apart from rows of Russian champagne lined up out of reach. It turned out to be quite tasty but would have cost a month's salary for any local.

A meal in a Russian restaurant was far from gourmet. There were designated places we could use our meal vouchers, and one, bleak Stalinist location with staff to match, refused to allow us in because we had missed our allotted time by just a couple of minutes. Negotiating with the staff, we were finally let in, only to discover the restaurant was completely empty, not because it was closed, simply because no one wanted to eat there. We soon found out why. When our 'meal' finally arrived, it was a revolting mass and a bowl disguised as thin soup. Even now, over 40 years later, I can honestly say it was by far the most inedible meal I ever had the misfortune to be served.

We got up and left, incurring further anger from the staff as we made a rapid exit for the car.

Heading back towards Finland we pulled into a bus shelter to secrete loose change in the crevices. These were roubles, the official currency of Russia, to be picked up by other Finns heading into the USSR. Importing or exporting currency was illegal, but the canny Finns had come up with a solution which worked.

It was a fascinating trip into a world of police and thieves, and so different to the Glasnost version I saw so many years later.

Chapter Sixteen :

Utrecht

Kodak had me presenting courses around the UK. In every business location there were departments booking me months ahead for training. I had become renowned for focusing on the behavioral and psychological impact of supportive teams which was groundbreaking stuff at the time. I was using Neuro-Linguistic Programming (NLP) and other skills to mentor and train senior staff and managers, and it was really paying off in terms of staff loyalty and satisfaction.

On one occasion I was up in Cumbria running an outward-bound type of team-building course when a senior IT guy confided he was on the verge of leaving Kodak. I knew at his level this would have been disastrous for the company, but at the same time he evidently had a lot of internal doubts about both the company and his own personal situation. I knew I couldn't leave him questioning every part of his life, so we travelled back by train together. For me giving this man my time wasn't work, it was my way of serving him at a time of need. We spent the five-hour journey counselling, coaching, and mentoring to draw out the decisions which were best for him. It laid the path for my life taking a different turn – but that comes later.

By this time, I had an excellent reputation across Kodak, and I was being asked to run programmes across the European network. The first destination was Utrecht, the company's training centre in the Netherlands.

The focus was again on team building and I gave them an exercise to complete in the late afternoon/early evening before we met for dinner. It gave me three hours of free time to take advantage of the swimming pool on the top floor of my city-centre hotel. Spotting the sauna, I had the usual crisis of an Englishman abroad – after my considerable time in Finland with Leila's family, I was used to a complete disrobe - but with no one around to define the dress code, I kept my shorts on.

After a brief time alone in the sauna, six to eight Germans arrived, a mix of young men and women, all butt naked. They settled around me on the benches and as often happens in a sauna, we got chatting and stayed in conversation until it was time to dress for dinner.

That evening Kodak staff were meeting at a barge restaurant moored on the river Rhine. Our group was seated at tables either side of the central walkway of the top deck and had just settled into small talk when the same group of Germans arrived and walked past us to get to their own table. As one of the girls stepped past me she stopped, did a double take, smiled and said "I didn't recognise you with your clothes on."

I shrugged – what more could I say?

My legend increased that night – and no amount of explanation would convince my colleagues of the complete innocence of her comment.

I arrived back in the UK from Utrecht and within a week or so was invited to meet with a trio of Germans from Kodak AG, the German subsidiary, to discuss a collaboration of talents.

Joachim Harder was an HR trainer, specializing in the benefits to the company of a highly skilled and motivated workforce. He had graduated from an eminent German university with a degree in psychology before moving to California to share and expand his skills in a healthcare setting. A few years later, by now in his late 20s, he was tempted back to Europe by an irresistible offer from Kodak.

Joachim was almost as tall as I was, slightly rotund, and thanks to early-onset hair loss inherited from his father, the first impression was of a merry and very capable tonsured monk. Back home in southern Germany I imagine he would have made a successful Burgermeister, bringing a town and its communities together, but instead he focused his skills and great intelligence on connecting with people. Although I was in my early 40s, and some thirteen years older than Joachim, we hit it off straight away.

The other two members of his hand-picked team were more reserved and kept themselves entertained, whilst Joachim and I bonded in our mutual love of adventure and travel. One thing I learned very quickly was that Joachim was far from risk averse.

Although representing Europe, Africa, and the Middle East (EAMA region), Joachim was based in the Kodak Hammersmith office and had a very attractive mews apartment tucked behind Harrods in Knightsbridge as his UK pied-à-terre. The place would have been worth millions even then, and it was all covered by Joachim's Kodak expense account, such was his value to the company.

After the meeting we repaired to a local hotel and then onto a restaurant in Chesham where we hashed out a plan to work together on a global training programme.

This was a huge turning point in my career and opened the flood gates to travelling around the world, teamed with Joachim, to offer exceptional training to Kodak's thousands of employees. More than this, it was the beginning of a lasting friendship which endures to this day.

Chapter Seventeen :

Cairo

I arrived in Cairo on a Sunday in 1990. As with all my business trips, the journey was taken out of season to make the best use of the Kodak company budget... and it was hot, so very, very hot and dusty. Just making it from the terminal to a cab left me dry and breathless.

The Rameses Hilton is positioned on the Nile Corniche, overlooking the great river about which I'd heard so much. The hotel was a modern oasis, clean and well appointed. Never had I been so glad to walk into an air-conditioned space! This was a real destination for visitors and businessmen alike.

The next morning, I needed to get to the Kodak office on 20 Adly Street. Knowing nothing of the city, taking one of the disorganised swarm of yellow and black taxicabs darting through the traffic to hover bee-like around the hotel was the only option. There were few private cars at that time, with the other road users being a chaotic smelly mixture of flatbed trucks, their cargo piled precariously high under tatty tarpaulin secured with frayed rope, and antiquated carts pulled by oxen and a few donkeys.

After 20 minutes of mayhem my driver turned down a dark, narrow street milling with people and animals and pulled up next to a street food stall where corn was being grilled. The smoke drifted upwards in an eye-stinging haze.

There was nothing to suggest this was the location for the office of a highly regarded multinational company, but when I questioned the cabbie, he pointed to a large dark doorway which looked more like the entrance of a menacing cave than any sort of business.

Once past the ground floor darkness, the building's ambiance improved significantly. The unexpectedly sumptuous offices were decorated with heavy dark wood furniture, all rather splendid and a far cry from the first impression. The Manager, Ravi Patel, was very welcoming. The obligatory refreshments arrived almost before I had taken a seat, because, as you know, a Brit survives on tea and biscuits!

With multiple training sessions booked this was a visit stretching over a couple of weeks. I was determined to make the most of the opportunity to learn more about the land of the Pharaohs in my precious free time. On the Saturday I walked onto a large square close to my hotel. To me it was a bustling and chaotic space with rather too many very young men in uniform carrying guns to protect the various government and diplomatic buildings. They didn't seem to have much in the way of training or discipline, and gave the impression of having a hair-trigger should anyone challenge them. It wasn't a place I was keen to hang around in, even then. Now Tahrir Square is remembered for other horrendous reasons after the violent suppression of protestors during the Egyptian revolution in 2011.

Back in 1990 and with a plan but no idea of my whereabouts or map to guide me, I stopped the first taxi I encountered.

Could the driver take me to the Antiquities Museum? He looked perplexed and checked that was where I really wanted to go. Was I sure?

I said yes, so he shrugged his shoulders, motioned me to get in and off we went. We drove three sides of the square, perhaps 80 metres per side and he stopped, motioning me to exit the cab.

Feeling suitably foolish, I paid him, got out and looked back at my hotel where the liveried doormen were clearly visible just a few minutes' walk away. The driver probably still recounts that story of the Englishman, too lazy to walk across the square!

The Cairo Museum of Antiquities resembled a vast Ikea store. It was huge and I was able to wander freely among the most amazing artefacts from thousands of years in Egyptian history.

There were no obvious restrictions stopping you from getting up close to the objects and very few were actually protected from the touch of enthusiastic tourists. It was probably just the sheer scale of the exhibits which prevented them from being stolen, because there really was nothing to stop that happening. There were just a couple of items which had more in the way of security – like the gold and lapis death mask of the boy king, Tutankhamen, which was kept out of reach in a sealed display case.

The place was hot and very dusty, not much of a destination for locals, and being out of season there were few people around. I was there for hours, drinking it all in and marvelling at the power of a civilisation which built pyramids and palaces, machinery, and government while the Brits were still living in the dark ages.

It came of something of a relief to hear the museum recently moved to new premises where these priceless objects, along with the mummies of the kings and queens of Egypt are now better cared for, and barring intervention, will continue to amaze for another millennia.

On Sunday I wanted to go to the pyramids at Giza just outside the city. Tour buses didn't operate on a Sunday when there weren't many visitors around, so climbing out of yet another taxi, all there was to behold on my arrival were a few camels, their guides and a handful of Egyptians standing around in anticipation of the few intrepid travellers who might make it out to the site.

How times have changed! Can you imagine no tourists whatsoever except for a lone Englishman? These days not even royalty could see the pyramids in such a unique way.

The guides wanted action and my presence inspired a bidding-war for trade. I was offered the opportunity climb up the main pyramid by a man dressed like everyone else in an ankle length beige djellaba and a smart red Fez cap. Aged around 30, tall and thin he welcomed me with open arms and promised me a 'secret route' to the top. How remarkable that after being there for thousands of years, my new best Egyptian friend was the only man in Egypt who knew this hidden path very nearly to the top of the Great Pyramid!

The Great Pyramid

The hand carved blocks which make up the resting place of Pharaoh Cheops are larger than they look in photos. Close to a metre square, there are small gaps which allow climbing between them, and my guide nimbly showed me the route through. As an engineer, the accuracy of the blocks and the way they had been put together fascinated me. Even with a basic understanding of how it might have been done after my visit to the Antiquities Museum, I couldn't conceive of the sheer industrial effort it took to create this and the other smaller pyramids, tombs, and temples of Egypt.

Part way up I stopped and looked at the view. At that moment, I reflected, we were just two tiny people standing alone on one of the most iconic structures in the world. It was an incredible feeling and one I would have dearly loved to share with Leila, but like many remarkable situations in my career, the majesty was consigned to memory and remains impossible to do justice in words.

I gather you'd probably be shot now if attempting to scale the Great Pyramid so I can't recommend you try it for yourself!

In the evening after the training sessions finished for the day I would walk along the Nile Corniche, just observing my surroundings. A few hundred metres up from the hotel was a second-hand car dealership outside which swung a sign proclaiming this was "Shady Motors". I mused this would have been a suitable sign for some UK dealers too.

On 'Barbeque night' I took my seat in the luxurious first floor restaurant right by the window. I could see the Nile glinting in the greying light across a patch of scruffy wasteland. Despite being the only diner, the chefs were keen to demonstrate their culinary skills and, despite my protestations, brought me an endless array of foods. Already satiated, I was surrounded by aromatic dishes I simply couldn't eat.

But outside, on the wasteland were a dozen or so people whose sole possessions were the clothes they stood up in. Desperately poor, they might not have eaten a decent meal in any form for a very long time.

The inequality of the situation left me cold. I found myself plotting a way to smuggle some of the food out of the hotel, but without the cover of other diners to distract the maître-d' and his staff, I would have been stopped before I reached the door.

Perhaps if I couldn't do it by stealth, I could be open about my intentions... but no. It was clear taking food to the homeless would have caused a riot and as word spreads fast, before the night was over, other 'vagrants' would come expecting to be fed. The hotel was well-aware of the emotional impact of starving people on the eyeline of tourists and had no intention of encouraging reliance on the charitable actions of guests, no matter how much food might go to waste as a result.

Reluctantly I could see their point; Cairo at night wasn't the friendliest of places, and accepting the hotel's perspective, I thought better of my plan. However, from then on in Cairo and in any other places where social inequality was rife, I made a practice of dropping low denomination notes to people sitting by the side of the road. Generally I chose women with babies and toddlers, but always doing so in a way which wasn't spotted by other beggars.

Chapter Eighteen :

Istanbul Taxi

My work for Kodak sent me back to the same places each year. It was easy to become blasé after visiting a city a couple of times. I was tall, confident and an experienced traveller, so the flights became almost like long bus rides and hopping into a taxi to go to the same hotel each visit was just routine.

On this particular occasion I arrived at Istanbul airport about 10:00pm. Back then it boasted a rather dark and tatty arrivals hall… nothing like the spectacular terminal the city now uses to welcome millions of tourists each year.

The sound of the cicadas hit me as I stepped out of the terminal into the stuffy night air. As usual I made my way to the unlit taxi rank. It was bustling with scruffy cab drivers and a jumble of cabs. Music was blaring from some, while others broadcast a football match with an excitable commentator describing the game to groups of drivers listening through open windows.

In other places I might have been met by a smartly suited driver with a town car, but not in Istanbul. There was no supervision of the drivers and it seemed anyone could turn up at the airport and pick up a fare. In other parts of the world, it wasn't unheard of for passengers and their luggage never to arrive at their hotel. Nevertheless, I wasn't fazed by the prospect of using a cab, and I really didn't have any other option.

Having been to the city several times, I knew the 20km direct route from the airport to the hotel. Abandoning conversation with my driver who evidently spoke no English, I settled back onto the sticky back seat and turned my attention to staring out of the window, imagining stepping into the cool air-conditioned foyer of my hotel, taking a refreshing shower and strolling out for a bite to eat at one of the many delicious family restaurants nearby.

I was shaken out of my visualization when the cab lurched and veered off the road onto a dirt track. My protestations were met by a fierce response from the driver. Dust and stones flying up alongside the car made seeing any landmarks along the pitch-dark road completely impossible. I had no idea where I was, what was going on or how I was going to get out of the situation.

Although I was vastly experienced as a traveller, it had never crossed my mind to learn how to escape a speeding car.

Terry Waite's capture and long solitary imprisonment in Beirut flew into my mind. He had hostage value as an envoy, but I didn't see myself as having the same diplomatic clout. Nevertheless, perhaps this man represented a group which understood more than I did about Kodak's influence in the area and how much they might be willing to pay for my return.

We raced down a winding track for what seemed like forever. It was probably only minutes, but the adrenalin rush had slowed time down while the fear of what was about to happen grew.

The road opened out into a little hamlet and the car slowed down. All the houses were shuttered, and the place seemed abandoned. Was I in one of the famous 'ghost villages' abandoned by entire populations fifty years earlier? I could hear dogs howling but other than that and the sound of the tyres grating across stone and gravel, silence.

The driver stopped abruptly by a two-storey house with stone steps up the outside wall. Like every other building it was dark, but he turned off the engine, ran up the staircase and disappeared out of sight.

I could feel myself shaking, mouth dry and my guts twisted into the tightest knot. I wondered if I'd ever see Leila and Sarah again, whether they would ever know what had happened to me. I looked out into the darkness sick to my stomach, could I bail out? How far would I get before he found me? Was he armed? Who had he gone to meet?

The back door was locked, but perhaps I could climb into the driver's seat and get out that way? It turns out being tall is a distinct disadvantage when trying to clamber out of a kidnapper's car. Before I'd worked out how I could fold and angle my body through the tight space, the sound of voices on the steps had me cowering back in my seat.

Glancing at the two men now standing outside the car, I noticed my driver holding a large box and smiling broadly at me. Shit. Was this what they would use to send me back to my family?

His companion gestured to me to open the window. Turning the handle and anticipating a gun being thrust through it, I opened it just an inch… like that would have made a difference! The man leant in towards me, his breath tainted with strong coffee and cigarettes…

"Thank you, thank you Sir. Sorry for delay. My brother he have to get birthday cake, take to family in Istanbul".

The driver got into the car, carefully placing his precious cargo on the passenger seat and shook hands with the translator before slamming the door and speeding on through the village.

Relieved and furious at the same time I gripped the seat to block against the lurching of the vehicle. We carried on along the same dirt track and soon rejoined the main road to the city. The lights of roadside restaurants and car dealerships were reassuring in a way I could never have imagined. Tears pricked my eyes, and I brushed them away angrily. Trying to hold in the nausea, I longed to hear Leila's voice, but at the same time, knew I couldn't call her in this state.

Our journey continued in silence. My driver was nonchalant, evidently pleased with himself for getting the English man to pay for his excursion into the countryside. I arrived at the hotel physically unscathed but emotionally on a knife-edge, my spirit and confidence shaken in ways it would take many months to recover.

Looking back on this, I translated an innocent, although thoughtless, decision on behalf of the driver into an attempted kidnapping and believed my life was on the line. With hindsight I had no evidence other than a detour from the main road to suggest malevolent intent, but news reports of businessmen, journalists and tourists taken for ransom in the Middle East and the issues with the Kurds and the PPK had created an underlying anxiety which came to the surface and overflowed that night.

It took a long while to see the bigger picture. I learned to step out of challenging situations to assess what is really going on. I knew the rest of the world wasn't as safe as my English home and in many areas, life is cheap. I became more aware and conscious that night and it served me well during my years in Russia.

Chapter Nineteen :

A Rough Ride

Peril, whether imagined or real, seemed to follow me around. Despite this, between regular international trips for work, it was essential to carve time out for rest and recreation with Leila.

Although self-contained and used to her own space, Leila was fascinated by my tales of travelling with Joachim and was inquisitive about what might now be described as our growing 'bromance'. Aware that I spent as much time hanging out with Joachim as I did at home with her, Leila wanted to meet him. Joachim was equally curious about this amazing woman who had captured my heart, and suggested we might team up for a holiday with Leila and his wife Maria.

Maria was a highly regarded PA at Daimler Benz. She was just over 5'10', a blonde with short, easily managed bobbed hair and an air of German efficiency about her. Maria's job meant she travelled a lot too, perhaps even more than Joachim, and they didn't see much of one another. The holiday was a great opportunity for us all to get to know one another better.

Our chosen destination was Chania in Crete, and in a bid to save money, Joachim selected a very traditional Greek hostel. The rustic accommodation was spartan and the concrete platforms were topped with thin mattresses masquerading as beds. The place scored low for both comfort and romance, and although the generous and hospitable Greek couple who owned it were friendly, Leila would have jumped at the opportunity to stay elsewhere.

We wanted to make the most of our visit to the largest of Greece's thousands of islands. It had become habit for Joachim and me to explore new areas on our own terms, so we hired an open top Suzuki 4-wheel drive jeep with the intention of traversing the mountainous central spine of the island to see the pink-tinted sands of Elafonissi Beach for ourselves. Joachim was always the pilot in left- hand-drive vehicles, while I took the wheel in countries where the steering wheel was on the right. He was confident and proud of his Teutonic driving skills.

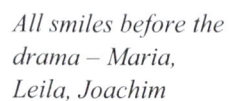

All smiles before the drama – Maria, Leila, Joachim

Travelling from the north coast and with no direct route to the remote beach, Joachim spotted a winding and very narrow dirt track heading south and took off up the hill. With no sat nav or map, and not for the first time in our friendship, we were launching into the unknown.

Any excursion with Joachim was likely to take us onto the road less travelled. I was sitting directly behind the driving seat looking out across rocky outcrops and dusty ridges when the road noise changed and the axle started to make rather odd grinding noises. Stones were ricocheting wildly, spitting against the underbody of the car and down into the barren valley below us. There was a definite sense of instability, a change in the air and atmosphere which gave me goosebumps despite the intense heat of the day.

The track had dwindled to almost nothing more than a goat path, and immediately to our left was a ravine with a sheer drop. I said nothing and leaned towards Leila to shift the jeep's centre of gravity further into the hill, knowing only a tiny fraction of the front and rear tyres could possibly be clinging to what was left of the road, while their outer edges were rotating in mid-air. Joachim was silent, I could see the tension in his neck.

Meanwhile the girls were chatting away in their accented English, sunglasses on and hair blowing in the breeze, totally oblivious to impending disaster.

I focused totally in the moment, helpless and mute, unable to speak for fear of distracting Joachim or betraying my intense fear. My only comfort was to position my body against Leila's tanned arm and thigh and knowing, if this was it, we would go together. I didn't dare clutch her hand, as much as I wanted to, she was astute enough to be aware something was wrong. Instead, I forced myself to breathe in and out for what felt like forever.

Somehow with a combination of skidding, luck and providentially located vegetation, the wheels managed to get purchase again and we continued on down the zig zag road to the harbour with only the two of us knowing how close a shave with certain death we had just experienced. Nauseous and sweaty, it was just another scrape we barely got out of alive.

Later, floating languidly on a boat on the sparkling Mediterranean, fortified by this time with several cold beers, I commented on our hairy mountain crossing. Maria said it had been perfectly safe, and as always, Joachim had shown his exceptional driving skills. Leaning towards me, a still shaken Joachim whispered under his breath "You and I know better!"

Chapter Twenty :

Kenya

On my first trip to Kenya I flew British Airways out of Heathrow and was pretty relaxed about arriving safely. You pass over spectacular scenery traversing the east coast of Africa whilst enjoying the onboard hospitality BA were famous for in the days before pre-packed M&S sandwiches.

Nairobi sits virtually on the equator and as we closed in on the city, it went from day to night almost instantly. With nothing to see outside, I was watching the screen above the seats in front of me as it indicated altitude and height above ground level.

The monitor showed we were still at over 6000 feet, but it was clear we were losing speed fast. My comfortable feeling disappeared. The cabin crew were going about their business and the other travellers were engrossed in books and screens, but after so many hours spent flying around the globe, I knew the plane was travelling too slowly to make a safe descent and landing. There was a long way to go, and my hand inched towards the call button to raise the alarm. Surely the cabin crew must have realised something was very wrong?

My anxiety grew and for what seemed like an age I fretted in my seat, trying to remember the drill for a crash landing, preparing to kick off my shoes and checking for the one hundredth time that my passport was in my jacket pocket. If I've learned anything from globetrotting, it's to always have your passport and wallet right there with you.

Suddenly there was a jolt and I truly believed this was it, my time had come. Darkest Africa was my nemesis and my mind's eye showed me the wreckage of a plane with no survivors. But then, from the depths of panic, my frazzled brain picked up on the sound of rubber on tarmac. We were down and cruising to a stop with the altimeter still showing 5800 feet. I might have been a seasoned traveler, but it never dawned on me that Nairobi sits on a plateau way above sea level.

Ironically this flight was not remotely dangerous, despite my unwarranted reaction, but a later one certainly made up for it.

Nearing Nairobi on my annual visit the following year, the Captain announced we were heading towards heavy weather and would need to avoid the worst of it. We could see a collection of towering white clouds from the ground to far above our current height. The mass, like a mountain range, was heavily spiced with some very black clouds.

As we were close to landing the sun should have been low on our right-hand side, out to the west, but it was a hard job keeping up with our route. Good job the pilot was on his game. One minute the sun was on our right and then suddenly on our left as he wove through the monster clouds. The plane was like a pinball in a machine, pinging around the sullen sky.

Typically British, no one said a word.

After what seemed like forever, but was probably no more than 20 minutes, the wheels safely kissed the tarmac at Nairobi Airport. Even the most stiff-upper-lipped amongst the passengers looked mightily relieved!

The hotel we used in Nairobi was a pleasant fifteen-minute walk across a small park from the central venue for our training. It was clearly prized by the city, being manicured, and carefully respected by the many locals making their way to work in the area. Taking the time to enjoy my surroundings was an important part of my day and I came to look forward to my 'commute.'

However, after work we would always take a taxi back to our hotel. Although it was only a five-minute drive, it was too dangerous to walk across this pretty space in the dark. Nairobi by night was not for the fainthearted.

Sometimes I needed to travel to the Kodak office which was some way out of the city.

This was a step back in time. The building was constructed in the 1930s and was a carbon copy of offices of the time in the UK. Brick construction with art-deco metal-framed Crittall windows, it could have been airlifted intact from a Surrey suburb. Even the toilets and sanitary ware had been shipped out from dear old Blighty – a visible reminder of the colonial past of the country.

On my first visit to the office, I noticed an unusual rattling sound coming my way. It's something you would never hear in the 21st century office - a lady in an overall tabard appeared at the door with a trolley of tea and biscuits. It was 3pm after all!

I'm sure by the 1990s the 'works tea trolley' was consigned to history back in England, but standards remained traditional for the team in Kenya. The essential tea and biscuits interval religiously punctuated every afternoon and they were always welcome.

The incongruity of this small enclave of little England was exacerbated by the view from the windows at the back of the office. A vast refugee camp stretched further than the eye could see. This displaced mass of humanity was living on the edge of the city in circumstances which, at best, would be described as squalid. I've no idea where they had come from, and the sight could have been straight from any news footage of war-torn Africa. It was heart-wrenchingly painful to witness.

Being a distant outpost of the Kodak empire, I don't think the company bigwigs knew or even cared about the devastation next door, but the local staff were Christian and made a point of doing all they could to improve the situation. The office manager, Mathias, was devout and gave much of his time and, I suspect, his income to the charities fighting to ease poverty and where he led, others followed. Kindness overflowed in that office, and they were truly a wonderful group of people.

HR was led by 'Resper', a joyous smartly dressed matronly lady in her 50s. She had much lighter skin than many of her colleagues; it was beautiful with not a crow's foot or wrinkle to be seen around her eyes and forehead. Her tall, straight, muscular frame, although solid, came across as angular and she was a lady who owned the room from the moment she opened the door. You wouldn't mess with Resper, but she would never give you reason to do so. She strongly disapproved of the double-standards of the men, especially her colleagues in the office, who were vocally Christian churchgoers on the outside, but targeted single women as 'friends with benefits', knowing it was a short step from prostitution in this male-dominated society.

Resper was caring and generous, especially to those out-of-town employees for whom evenings in a hot hotel room could be very demoralizing. Whether for distraction from temptation, or through a genuine desire to make us welcome, she invited Joachim and me to join her and her two children for dinner at her home in a suburb of the city some 10km from the office.

I don't know quite what I'd expected, but as we travelled through a run-down area of the city, the truth of my detached brick-built luxury back in the UK really hit home. Resper and her family lived in a two-storey mud walled house on a scruffy lot on a street of similar homes.

To British eyes, what looked like the most basic of living accommodation was middle class by black African standards. As a professional woman, Resper employed a live-in housekeeper to take care of the children and her neat home, whilst she earned a living working for Kodak. She regarded it as her economic responsibility to support her community by providing work and the dignity of employment for others.

The housekeeper had prepared a meal in the traditional tall African charcoal stove along with two tall, round earthenware pots nestled into the ground. It was simple, as authentic as it comes and absolutely delicious. I thought of my well-equipped kitchen back home and realised this meal was as good as anything I'd eaten anywhere else in the world.

There was no doubt spending time in Nairobi with its colonial undercurrent and the juxtaposition between rich whites and poorer blacks was a real clash of environments.

The Kodak managers were a sociable bunch, and we were often invited to great bars with them in the evenings. They were always enthusiastic hosts, and we were the only whites who ever went out with them. They all had girlfriends (usually several) at these bars, as well as being married. The cultural difference between us caused great confusion when they asked how many girlfriends I had back home and I replied "None, I am married", blurring my relationship status in a way they would understand. Nevertheless, they found this bemusing and quite incomprehensible – I wasn't considered unattractive, and, in comparison to my companions, I was wealthy and deserved to have many beautiful ladies to admire me. How could it be that one woman was enough? All I can say is, they didn't know Leila!

In contrast to the bars the Kodak team went to regularly, we tried out a couple of the more famous bars which were featured in the guidebooks. These turned out to be basic beyond belief. To order a beer, you queued at a heavily grilled bar to pay. A single bottle would be handed through a gap just big enough to avoid spilling the contents. There were no glasses, but this turned out to be the most hygienic option because the rest of the interior was grim. There was nowhere to sit, and the toilets were beyond belief. Even in the most desperate of situations, it would be preferable to go in the street than use the filthy lavatories offered by this 'famous' establishment. Understandably I wasn't in any hurry to go back.

The western-themed 'Buffalo Bill's' had a dance floor with tables and many attractive African girls who saw travellers as a commodity. You didn't need to be in the bar long before a very forthright woman would present a list of the sexual favours on offer.

To be honest, it was inevitable travelling internationally for work that the places I stayed in would attract women who had been pushed into or chosen prostitution as a profession. In Moscow you got the impression it was very much a career choice, with high class escorts enjoying the benefits of top hotels and restaurants, but in other places, like Nairobi, it was not so much a choice as a decision made in desperation.

There in Buffalo Bill's a polite and sweet looking very young girl approached us. She was dressed in her finest and could have been on her way to school or church... instead she gave us, in the most explicit terms, an option to fill any orifice. There was no introduction, no conversation, no enquiry as to our interest, just a blunt menu of her wares. I was shocked by the openness, and all these years later I still am. The oldest profession thrives wherever businessmen congregate, but this was by far the most blatant and disturbing example I ever experienced...

This was the 1980s and the Aids epidemic, which was to cause so many African lives to be lost, was just starting to be talked about. None of us wanted anything to do with these ladies of the night, but everywhere we went, they followed.

Sunday was always the brightest day of the week because everybody appeared in their "Sunday best" to go to church. The women were colourfully attired, and each wore the mandatory hat while the children did their best to respect their elders whilst constricted in a rainbow selection of fabrics and frills. The men were smart too in conventional dark suits and ties, while many wore a trilby or homburg hat to finish off the outfit.

Outside the church it was a kaleidoscope of colour and extremely busy. Church services were a cacophony of praise, preaching and song and went on for hours. Some churches had open sides to manage the intense heat and you would see the ladies fanning themselves while children tried not to fidget.

I bet vicars in the UK would like to have a congregation like that every Sunday.

Chapter Twenty-One :

Safari Sunset

Once a year my colleague and great friend Joachim would join me to run our annual courses in Kenya. Making the most of our time in this great country, we regularly stayed on to go on safari. Taking a taxi out of town to Wilson airfield, the old national airport, we flew in an ancient Dakota DC3 to a landing strip in the Masai Mara.

The first time, however we hadn't really thought it through. A local travel agent booked our four-day trip, and I have to say it was much cheaper for us than the average adventurer! We had already done the international flight and an African colleague negotiated an extremely competitive deal for us… it was cheaper to spend four days on Safari at a glamorous compound than it would have been to eat in Nairobi over the weekend.

The only challenge we had were the hard-shell suitcases we used to traverse the world – great for a businessman with training materials to transport – but totally unsuited to the limited cargo hold of the elderly plane built for use by the RAF back in the second world war.

In a last-minute panic, we transferred a limited amount of kit into flimsy white hotel laundry bags and left the executive luggage in storage.

Most of our fellow passengers looked as though they had arrived from the set of 'Out of Africa' or 'The African Queen'. It was all Louis Vuitton, khaki, and knee length shorts.

Wilson airfield didn't boast anything as exotic as baggage handlers, you had to hand your bags up to the crew leaning precariously out of the hold. Joachim and I made a great play of handing over our 'exclusive' laundry bags and the crew responded by treating them as though they contained the most precious cargo. I'm not sure the other travellers were that impressed, but it made us laugh.

The flight to Masai Mara was around 30 minutes, bumping through thermal currents above the hot savannah with a bird's eye view of grazing herds of antelope and wildebeest. The landing strip was bare earth, and a cloud of dust trailed the antique DC3 as it set down in the wild. In keeping with our departure, our bags were carefully lowered into our waiting arms whilst our companions tutted at our brash behaviour.

Nurturing our bags, we stepped into a new, bright, and exciting world.

'Arrivals' at Masai Mara comprised a couple of stalls where local crafts were being sold by two statuesque female Masai warriors. It might come as a surprise to know both men and women are regarded as warriors in this remarkable tribe. These women could have finished us off without thinking about it – instead they gave us a masterclass in sales techniques.

Their potential customers, mainly American women of a certain age and style, clearly believed they knew about value for money and assumed the Masai did not. Having spent a little time in Africa I stood to one side and watched poker-faced for around 20 minutes as the price was bartered upwards. The final prices agreed were heavily in favour of the sellers, and yet those American ladies believed they had achieved the bargain of the century. A good lesson to learn, never challenge a Masai – in combat or shopping!

We had the pleasure of staying at Little Governors Camp, which somehow managed to be quite luxurious and primitive in equal measure. The main lodge was very impressive, a big circular building with great beams stretching up and meeting at the apex of the roof, poised over a central fireplace. We ate and socialized there and on the adjacent grassy area which had a swimming pool, barbeque and, like any other resort, sunbeds, although it paid to examine them carefully for snakes and scorpions before sitting down!

However tastefully appointed the camp was, it was hard to describe the sleeping quarters as anything more than 'basic.'

Little Governor's Camp, in the Masai Mara

On one visit we were accommodated in a tent right beside a path which led from the Mara river far beyond the camp and inland onto the plains. The tent pegs were right beside the path which initially seemed like rather a duff idea.

Not so however, it turned out this was a hippo track which these enormous and unpredictable beasts followed nightly to go foraging inland during the hours of darkness. They would return to the river at daybreak and woe betide any man found on their path.

Hippos are responsible for more human deaths in Africa than any other wild animal, and many Africans meet their maker after getting on the wrong side of a hippo.

So here we were at the Little Governors' Camp with our tents on one side of the path and the communal toilet block on the other. Now it began to make sense that the pegs and guy ropes were positioned with care to help the hippos stay on their beaten track and out of our modest tent… however, the distance to the bathroom was something of an issue for men of a certain age who have perhaps imbibed more than may be wise during the long, warm African evening.

The team at the camp had learned the hard way about coming between a hippo and its intended destination so a 'crossing patrol guy' was stationed outside our tent each night to shepherd us across the path in safety, should the need arise.

One particular night in the gloom of our shared tent, I was ill at ease without knowing why and repeatedly stretched my hand out to touch the ground sheet. Joachim, trying to sleep nearby, and nervous of the unexpected attention, quite reasonably wanted to know why I persisted in making these gestures in his direction.

I told him I just wanted to be sure I knew where my torch was, that was all. He could relax, I wasn't making advances. I turned my torch on to demonstrate and there in the pool of light between us was a small bright yellow and black frog. This little reptile was super toxic to humans and enough to cause a lot of pain if inadvertently touched or trodden on. These nasties are hopping danger signs for good reason and, had either of us got up in the dead of night, the little bugger would have been in prime position to do maximum mischief.

Diverting the hippo guard to remove our unwelcome guest, Joachim turned over and was soon snoring as only a dashing German can. I meanwhile clutched my torch tightly in my sleeping bag, wondering what other creatures might find our company irresistible!

*

Each morning at 5am, just before dawn, with the starlit darkness still twinkling across the heavens, a waiter would materialize outside the tent, gently waking us with the words 'Jambo, good morning'. Then, setting a tray of freshly brewed coffee on the terrace table, he would leave us to our grunting, farting and groaning ablutions. It may be said that a middle-aged man's similarity to a mature warthog is even more astonishing when shared in their natural savannah habitat. Joachim, of course, blamed me for the racket, but I couldn't possibly comment for fear of causing an international incident.

For Joachim and me, the early alarm call, whilst charming in itself, felt a little cruel after a surfeit of gin and tonics the night before.

Breakfast was always a great start to the day – very 'Downton Abbey' with pristine tablecloths, an impressive English style breakfast and excellent service.

Unlike your average table however, we didn't have dogs or cats circling the table for tidbits. Here a different animal had made a habit of joining the guests and meals were accompanied by a chorus of mum and her baby wild pigs, grunting, sniffing and snuffling around our legs.

One afternoon, whilst taking tea at three, (which remained a tradition in Africa long after the English had moved on to other things) Joachim and I were relaxing in deckchairs just outside our tent. Suddenly an uproarious rabble of baboons, a troop around 50 strong, pelted through the camp screaming and shouting as they ran riot through the place tipping over anything which got in their way. Completely unconcerned by the two of us watching open mouthed, they behaved like a mass of football hooligans rampaging through a city centre. At this point I had no idea of the damage a full-grown baboon could inflict on a human, and that was probably a good thing, as instead I simply sat still and observed the similarities between primate and human behaviour.

Each day the camp would line up Land-Cruisers to take tourists out into the reserve in convoy. Never liking to follow the crowd, Joachim and I would convince our game-guide to head off in another direction so we could do our own thing. Being on our own away from the loud 'oohs and aahs' of excited or complaining Americans meant we saw amazing animal behaviour which would otherwise have been missed.

On a bend in the Mara river where the water scours the outside of the bank and leaves a small beach on the slower moving side, we were perhaps three metres above the river on a sandy cliff looking down on three Nile crocodiles sunbathing on their private beach. These reptiles are huge, the length of two family-sized cars, and had we been within striking range we wouldn't have stood a chance against them. However, there we were, taking in the extraordinary power of nature in this beautiful and deadly country.

Returning to the camp one evening we had to cross the raging Mara river. It was 'short rains' season – there are short rains around November and a longer period of rains in the spring. Guides were helping us into a rather small wooden boat when I noticed a dark brown snake riding the floodwater, its head and upper body rearing up out of the water. Pointing it out to the guides, they, as a man, leapt for the riverbank leaving us stranded in the dinghy... they said it was harmless, but that didn't seem to fit with the fear in their eyes!

One morning, for a change, we took a walking tour and set off into the savannah with a Masai warrior armed only with a very short stick. It occurred to us to be marginally surprised, after all the game guides carried rifles and dart guns, but we figured he probably knew what he was doing.

Scrambling to the top of a small outcrop of rocks we discovered a rhino and calf just a few metres away from the ridge. If I'd been home in Hertfordshire, I wouldn't have wanted to be this close to a domesticated cow and calf let alone this enormous armour-clad beast with a horn which could have torn us in two.

"No problem" gestured our guide, walking quietly off in the other direction…

*

Joe was our regular driver, and if it was just Joachim and me out on safari, we would stand in the Toyota Land Cruiser looking ahead to survey our domain. Joe joked we were like Rommel and Montgomery in a tank! We were striking a pose and moving forward in unison. How different our connection would have been just a generation earlier, when our parents and grandparents were at war.

Starting out after a rainy night, the paths were wet with occasional puddles. Joe carefully manoeuvered the Toyota through the fragile landscape, protecting the unique ecosystem as best he could. Although many off-road vehicle paths exist, the guides are careful not to create unnecessary new ones.

This morning however, part of the road had become a lake, there was no safe way to go through it because the depth and subsurface were unpredictable. We were miles away from regular routes, so putting ourselves in a position where rescue was required was both dangerous and stupid. Instead, Joe diverted into an adjacent meadow. As the saying goes, Big mistake – huge!

Joachim and I were huddled in the back seat, dressed entirely inappropriately for the unexpected chill in the early morning air, when the Landcruiser lurched and became stuck in squelching, gloopy mud. Our disappointing day just got a whole lot worse.

Of course, Joachim helpfully declared that had our chariot been an original British Land Rover rather than a Japanese knock-off, it would never have been trapped in the first place. Meanwhile, ignoring the futile comments of his commanders, Joe tried out all the gears and differential locks on the vehicle without success.

Finally, Joe turned to 'Rommel and Montgomery' and suggested that at least one of us, and preferably both, get out of the cruiser and push. Since 'Rommel' was already at a disadvantage, having lost the war, Joachim crawled out of the back seat, and shivering, braced himself against the back of the vehicle. Slowly, knee deep in the mudhole and channelling the might of the Desert Fox, Joachim propelled us out of the quagmire and back onto solid ground.

Joe and I were still applauding and cheering our muck-spattered companion as we accelerated back onto the path. Even the sun peered out from behind the clouds and a heard of antelope crossed our way in celebration of 'Rommel's' victory against the elements and the welcome recommencement of our safari. Joe's thanks were uncharacteristically effusive, mentioning Rommel's 'courage and determination'. As Joe was a man of few words, this made 'Montgomery' somewhat suspicious, so I asked Joe why he hadn't put one of us behind the wheel and pushed the car out himself?

"Snakes" he replied, his eyes wide open with dread and undisguised panic in his voice.

Right there we learned another lesson, on no account ever paddle in an African puddle!

*

My most precious memory of our safari days was the culmination of one glorious safari and an evening barbeque on a ridge with a view over the rippling grassland and scrubby trees of the plains.

As the staff busied themselves preparing the food, I found myself standing in that warm, calm evening looking to the west as the sun set in a vast orange glow on the horizon. It was indescribably beautiful.

I became aware Joachim had come to stand on my left and a Masai in full tribal regalia flanked my right. We stood silently, comfortably, lost in the spectacle of this shared inspiring and intense moment.

It was a big moment in my life, one of the most joyous and connected experiences in my time on earth. I often find myself there in my thoughts, even now, many decades later.

The world could learn from taking in the majesty of such moments in time.

Chapter Twenty-Two :
Johannesburg

I was met by one of the Kodak secretaries at the airport at the beginning of my first visit to South Africa. She was designated as my driver until a car could be organised and I 'got the hang' of the place. It was 1992 and apartheid was still in full force.

The city was regarded as dangerous, although life went on just as it would in any major city, my mini skirted companion drove with a gun between her thighs. She made it clear she would have no hesitation in using it should the need arise.

She was in her early twenties, smartly attired for her corporate role. Her slim shape, vivid blue eyes and north European colouring were enhanced by her golden tan. Everything about her, from the salon fresh hair and manicure to the confident handling of the pistol screamed entitled white girl, and she made no secret of her belief she and other members of the Afrikaans community had superiority over the black population.

Like all people her age she had been trained in the use of firearms from an early age and educated me in how to shoot through a closed window without the bullet ricocheting back into the car. Some things you learn and wish you hadn't.

That pick up at the airport was the first time I'd ever seen members of the public carrying guns on the street.

Mike and Joachim with staff at Kodak Johannesburg

Even something as simple as going out for a Chinese meal in a very ordinary location was complicated by booking ahead and negotiating the parking area. Once you'd got past a security gate where guards checked you were permitted to be there, the car park was patrolled by armed guards to protect diners and the restaurant staff. There seemed to be no opportunity to just relax and enjoy a meal without the tension of being surrounded by guns.

We stayed in an up-market area called Santon which was very Californian in appearance and attitude. It boasted high class restaurants and exclusive stores but was some distance from the Kodak offices in the centre of town.

On one occasion I became a little blasé about the drive back to Santon and misjudged the exit, coming off the freeway early and accidentally taking the road to Alexandria, a notorious township. I drove 100 metres in and realised the error of my ways. We knew cars were taken at gunpoint in this area and stripped down for parts. The occupants were fodder – the local gangs had no hesitation in shooting anyone who didn't turn and walk away the way they had come.

As I drove, more eyes were on the car than was comfortable. We could feel the menace seeping in around the tightly closed windows. Finding the first place to spin the vehicle, I was out of there so fast the tyres were smoking.

Both Joachim and I loved life in the fast lane, but this was one route I had no interest in taking again.

Looking for an escape from the pressure-cooker atmosphere of being visitors in Johannesburg, Joachim and I had the great idea of driving to the famous luxury resort, Sun City, for a weekend break, rather than spending money on the short flight anyone else would have chosen. This was a journey of about 4 hours, and experience made it clear there was no stopping on the route! We were approaching crossroads in the middle of nowhere and flying straight over to avoid stopping or even slowing down. No matter how tempting it was to stop at one of the roadside stalls, statistics suggested the fruit sellers were more likely to rob us or worse, than sell a banana. My English sensibilities could not equate why a man who made a business on a roadside stall would need a Kalashnikov, but this was South Africa in the 1980s and sensibilities didn't come into it.

When we got back to work the following Monday the Afrikaners thought we were mad to even consider the journey. We were probably the only whites driving without firearms in the whole of South Africa.

Chapter Twenty-Three :

Kigali

Heading home, my flight left Johannesburg International Airport after 10pm. In African terms this was late in the evening and the continent was sleeping as the plane hit cruising height of around 37,000 feet.

There were no lights, nothing to see and we settled in for the six-hour flight time along the spine of Africa, oblivious to the borders of the countries below.

Around two hours in, there was a ripple of sound through the cabin. Far below were fireworks – a lot of fireworks and some seemed to be heading in our direction.

This was something of a surprise. Africa wasn't known for pyrotechnic displays.

At that point the captain's voice came calmly over the tannoy to explain we were crossing Rwanda, at that time experiencing a vicious civil war between the Tutsi and Hutu factions. It seemed the Rwandan army was firing rockets skyward in an effort to quell the rebellion. I'm not clear whether it did any good on the ground, but it certainly made it somewhat uncomfortable mid-flight.

However, the Captain was reassuring, "They have nothing which will go above 10,000 feet – we're fine and safe up here". All the same, I think we all breathed a sigh of relief when the 'fireworks' faded into the distance, and I idly wondered how our British Airways captain could be so sure the armies hadn't been restocked by the Russians or any other military superpower.

Chapter Twenty-Four :

Budapest

For a while during my time with Kodak I was seconded to EAMA and each year my travels would take me on a circuit across the EAMA regions... Europe, Africa, The Middle East and Asia.

Budapest was a regular destination and after a while each visit blended into the next.

Staying in Óda Buda (Old Budapest) it was decided we should have a dinner out with a dozen Kodak employees, and booked a gypsy-style taverna with full on violinists and superb food. It was a fabulous experience, and we were all relaxed and enjoying the evening when there was a commotion by the door.

Everyone in the restaurant turned to see what was going on. There was a small group of people led by someone who seemed vaguely familiar – he was furious, demanding in English to be taken to the table he had reserved. Although it was evident every table was taken, he could not understand why these inept Hungarians were denying his group access and became ruder and more obnoxious with every sentence. His voice got louder, and his body language was saying everything. Even his party looked uncomfortable. The more he said, the more familiar he seemed. Ready to leave and somewhat embarrassed by this rude Englishman, we picked up our coats and headed towards the door. Only then did I realise just who this unpleasant character was, and, to his horror at being recognised, said "Good evening Mr. X". Out of kindness, I will just say he was a renowned political presenter, and I lost all respect for him after seeing him exhibit behaviour of the type he would never condone on his own show.

Spending a lot of time in Budapest and many other international cities over the years, I'd reached the conclusion it was no fun sitting in a hotel room at night, especially when a gang of Kodak employees were all in the same boat. It made sense to go out and experience the culture of the places we were staying in.

Down on the Pest side of the Danube, we were whiling an early evening away as a group when someone decided it was time for a drink and led us into the nearest bar. The thing was, this bar was very dark, and it took a few moments to (using a Kodak term) 'get our eyes'. Feeling our way through the almost pitch black we were seated at a table and as our eyes acclimatized to the gloom, we realised every waitress was as naked as the day they were born. Seconds later we understood they weren't backward in coming forward either.

These chatty, extraordinarily attractive women plonked themselves in our laps and were encouraging us to get to know them better. They clearly did not believe in a 'hands off' approach.

Now I'd love to say that we left immediately – but that wouldn't be true. Some of our companions were clearly enjoying the attention and were in no hurry to move on. Joachim and I made an informed decision to focus on drinking the night away. However, that wasn't what my 'new best friend' still seated on my lap, had in mind.

With her excellent English, our conversation flowed. As a restrained Brit, I tried to focus on her face and blot out the fact that a stunningly attractive blonde was sitting on my knee, but it had already dawned on me that this lady was not a waitress at all. Clearly intent on reeling in her catch, she indicated a sign on the wall, and invited me to read it aloud – 'Masturbation Room'. By this time, I was very drunk and somewhat giggly. I asked what were the fees to go into the room?

"Fifty dollars" she replied "a bargain, do you want to go ahead? Let's go upstairs".

She hopped off my lap and tugged on my arm, pointing towards the door.

I stayed put and feigned confusion…

"Well hang on a moment" I said, "When do I get my \$50?"

I thought it was hysterical, in only the way a very drunk man would see it. Joachim was laughing too. My companion didn't seem to share the joke and flicked her finger in the direction of the security guards. Our whole group was bundled to the exit and thrown out onto the street by some of the biggest bouncers I've ever seen.

The young lads probably dined out on it for years; certainly it became one of Joachim's favourite anecdotes about our time working together.

Joachim Harder

145

Chapter Twenty-Five :

Saudi Arabia

With the second Gulf War still reverberating around the Middle East, my first visit to Saudi Arabia turned out to be an unexpected glimpse into the world of the Saudi elite.

Throughout the Kodak years flying to various parts of the world was a weekly activity and with a sharp eye on the budget, I was always seated in economy. My flight to Jeddah became immediately out of ordinary as I was invited to take my seat in the very luxurious First-Class upper cabin of a Saudi Airlines jet. It crossed my mind I could easily get used to this!

With a team of four extremely attentive cabin crew for the small group of privileged passengers, the hours between London and the desert kingdom flew by. I was relaxed in my seat and frankly in no hurry to move after the plane touched down. It made sense to wait until everyone else had exited and enjoy the comfort for a few minutes more.

With a murmur of voices and averted eyes, a casually dressed man appeared beside me, asked my name and said, "come with me". I thought "Uh oh, I'm in trouble here" but had no idea why. Was this man here to arrest me or was I being abducted? It didn't look good.

He escorted me off the plane and through immigration while other passengers were held back while we passed. On into the opulent baggage hall, an official took a casual look at my documents before I was hustled past queues of waiting Saudi's, through a side gate and out of the airport.

"My bags?" I asked, wondering if I was going to need them wherever he was taking me. "Just coming" he replied. "I'm taking you to your hotel".

It turned out I was receiving VIP treatment, and the mystery man was my driver-cum-fixer-cum-guide for the trip. He was an employee of the Saudi prince who had set up a joint venture arrangement with Kodak and evidently valued my services rather more than my employer ever had!

How the other half live.

After a few days of running a detailed training programme in my lavish hotel, I was invited to the residence of the Prince and his family.

I'd been invited into the homes of Kodak employees and partners around the world, but this was a new level. The palace was huge, ornately decorated and wildly excessive. Funnily enough, my clearest recollection is of an enormous white leather sofa which stretched around three sides of the receiving room and would have accommodated a dozen lounging men with lots of room to spare.

The Prince and I settled to conversation until his wife and teenage daughter arrived to join us. In accordance with religious convention, the women were covered from head to foot by their black boshiya, the local term for the outer garments more generally known as a burka.

Once they were inside and the door closed behind them, the two pulled off the black fabric to reveal jodhpurs, polished riding boots, dress shirts and jackets. They could have stepped out of the pages of 'Country Life' and would have blended seamlessly into the home-counties upper class set. My bewildered expression resulted in hoots of laughter, and they hurried to put me at my ease.

Once introductions had been made, the Princess said, "I need a drink" and stepped across the room to a cupboard to pour herself a generous glass of Johnnie Walker Black Label. She laughed again at my surprise and handed me a tumbler full of the one liquid I hadn't expected to see until I returned to the UK.

The prince, evidently in thrall to his wife, said he'd have a whiskey too. "No" she said, poking his arm "you will not!"

Isn't life intriguing? He might have been a prince, but within the walls of that home, that princess definitely wore the trousers.

Conversation turned to the ways in which alcohol found its way into the 'dry' realm of Saudi Arabia. It seems the 'diplomatic bag' is less a battered satchel full of documents, and more along the lines of a shipping container stacked with crates of whatever tipple takes the fancy.

Just as the expats living in protected compounds and gated communities sunbathed, boozed and behaved exactly as they would on the beaches of the Algarve, the less devout Saudis were partial to a G&T sundowner or champagne reception and had no problem obtaining the finest brands... helped along the way in a 'you scratch my back' arrangement with diplomatic teams based in embassies from around the globe.

The shopping experience was altogether more strange. Like any westernized department store, you'd walk into a plethora of gilded perfume counters and displays of high end make up, but with strict regulations preventing women from working, they were entirely staffed by men. If I got the opportunity, I'd always return home with a little something for Leila, and her preference was always for beautiful fripperies. The Jeddah lingerie showroom was three times the size of any I'd seen in Europe or America, but again, while Saudi women could shop with a male chaperone, the salespeople were all men. Mindboggling!

The dress code, whilst restrictive for local women, was looser for internationals. It wasn't unusual to see foreigners wandering around in western dress; although mini-skirts, bare arms and shorts were definitely out of the question, and arrest would have followed.

My second visit to the Kingdom saw me based in Riyadh which was infinitely more conservative than Jeddah had been.

My hotel was in the outskirts of the city on a main route to war-torn Iraq. It was a non-descript place, more of a business hotel and not remotely special to look at.

Waiting outside the hotel one morning for my delayed taxi to arrive, I noticed a peculiar, cylindrical shape on the other side of the road. With nothing better to do, I wandered across to find something which looked rather like a large, dirty green crumpled Christmas cracker. A little light questioning revealed this was one of Saddam Hussein's scud missiles, 37ft long and around 3ft wide it had been aimed at the Saudi city but fell short and landed at the roadside.

Weaponry was certainly bigger since Hitler's attempt on my life with a doodlebug.

I had other observations whilst staying in the city. When a family ate out, the men would go to one restaurant while the women and children went to another. They were completely segregated, and it made for a very different atmosphere in the city.

A square in the centre of town was aptly named "Chop Chop Square" by local expats. This was where miscreants, the men and women accused of adultery, theft, murder, and lesser crimes were punished or executed early on Friday mornings before the square was hosed down and 'prayer day' began. It was very much represented as a public display and the expat community was strongly encouraged to attend in order to imply their support for the brutal activities which took place there.

I did visit the square, but not on a Friday. I was all too aware of the gruesome history of beheadings and crucifixions taking place there and which continue to this day. What might have been acceptable in Europe in the grisly middle-ages certainly didn't fit my perception of justice in the 1990s, and it was an uncomfortable atmosphere which stayed with me long after my return to the UK. I chose not to return to Riyadh and found it difficult to understand the contrast between the friendship offered by the Prince and Princess in Jeddah and the horrific atrocities routinely perpetrated in a city in the same country.

Chapter Twenty-Six :

Aerostar Hotel 1991

My first visit to Moscow occurred whilst I was working for Kodak. We were staying at the Aerostar hotel, so called because of its position next to old Moscow international airport of Khodyskoe Pole in the Begovoy district in the Northwest of the city. The airport had gone out of service some 40 years earlier.

The old airfield was being used as a compound for old aircraft. This was the abandoned hardware of the Soviet air force, along with enough military equipment to start a war dumped with no more security than a chain link fence and a few guards who were more than ready to turn a blind eye.

I was sitting at the bar one night with a couple of colleagues, one of whom had arranged for us to 'visit' the site with the assistance of a local man. All we had to do was cross the hotel car park, which sounds simple, but was the biggest challenge of the whole outing. The snow had started to thaw during the day and become slushy but since sundown everything had frozen into solid ridges and potholes in the −20°C of the Moscow night. We struggled to make our way across, slipping, tripping, and sliding towards a hole in the chain link fence.

Our 'tour guide' in the smart uniform of a serviceman, beckoned us in from the other side and just like that, we were exploring a space where no Brits should ever have been.

But we weren't just looking! I found myself sitting in the cockpit of a Mig 15 – a remnant of the Korean war and well past its sell-by-date which, from memory, had been the bane of American planes during the conflict. These war machines had done so much damage, but up close it was beyond me how they could have been so ruthlessly efficient. The plane was made up of any number of small clumsily riveted plates and the instrument panel was more basic than that of a moped. If you'd told me it had been made of recycled baked bean cans I wouldn't have been surprised. It must be testament to the design that this plane had outperformed and outmanoeuvred the power of the American air force so successfully and with such devastating consequences.

My next piece of equipment was a two-seater interceptor helicopter with the most peculiar windscreen arrangement which looked rather like a half-blown bubble. My recollection is that it was an E155M model used for reconnaissance, it certainly didn't have a gun turret or any obvious fixings for guns or bombs.

After an hour in the freezing night, we were all ready to slip back unnoticed through the fence. Just before we crossed back into the perilous car park, we handed over the 'fee' for our night's entertainment – a packet of cigarettes. The Russian military obviously knew the end was in sight for the regime, even if the government wasn't willing to admit it.

Chapter Twenty-Seven :

Sun and Fun in Siberia

During my time in Moscow, I was asked to run a training programme in Novosibirsk, a Siberian city about halfway to the eastern coast at Vladivostok which is the third largest city in Russia. It's hard to quantify the sheer scale of Russia, but to try to give the journey some context, London is closer to Moscow than my training destination – there were more time zones to cross than I care to remember.

Like the wide-open farming states of America, the Siberian plains were bitterly cold in winter and uncomfortably hot in the summer. This was August and the temperature was above 30°c.

This was a straightforward internal flight, four hours from Moscow – the equivalent of flying from London to Greece but with fewer holidaymakers.

Looking down from the plane, the terrain was endless, hundreds upon hundreds of miles of flat, featureless expanse stretching further than the eye could see or have the heart to look for. Arriving in Novosibirsk in the early evening was a pleasant surprise. The city centre was quite modern, even welcoming, although the suburbs were comprised of the inevitable grey, depressing Stalin blocks.

My hotel was definitely on a par with western hotels, another happy surprise as many of my destinations were more gulag than gracious.

After unpacking my bags, I found my way to the large communal dining hall for my evening meal. Restaurants weren't really on the menu in 90s Russia, intimate dining and subdued lighting were still way in the future and even in top hotels, the food service resembled a works canteen or vast school dining room.

The place was thronged with a wedding party and when one of the guests realised I was English I was press-ganged into joining them. How exciting to have an exotic visitor to toast.

If you've never been to a Russian wedding, and this was my first, there are certain traditions to uphold.

It started with someone toasting me with the inevitable vodka, which of course, had to be downed-in-one. I then had to toast him back – another vodka. Every man in the room wanted to repeat the process, each making an effusive welcome to the stranger in their midst while I mumbled something back. The more vodka I drank, the louder and more enthusiastic I became. I had no idea what they were saying to me any more than they could comprehend the booming voice of the Englishman.

Around the room were small round glass topped tables, each decked with glasses, vodka, and Russian champagne. The place was swimming in alcohol; this wedding was definitely 'no expense spared', and they hadn't wasted time on bar staff, if you wanted another glass, you poured it, and then another … and another.

As none of the women had ever met an Englishman, my next responsibility was to dance with each of them – from the most beautiful, to the dourest rattling babushka. Thankfully my time in Russia had given me a strong head for booze and I managed to stay upright, and (I hope) relatively charming for the duration. Quite an introduction to Novosibirsk!

The next morning, feeling utterly dreadful, I started my training programme with an apology for not feeling 100%. "No problem" declared a student "It's fine, all normal for Siberia."

Making the most of the time in Novosibirsk, a midweek dinner was planned for the trainees on the course. We were to visit a large sauna facility known as a 'Banya'.

One of the Kodak secretaries was given the task of organizing the meal, with the assistance of a young woman from a local events company. Finalising the arrangements for the food and copious alcohol, the events woman asked, "How many girls do you need?"

Miss Kodak, having heard it all before, answered that this was Kodak, and the company didn't do that.

When we arrived for dinner, the selection of beds stacked unceremoniously at the end of the dining hall and the glowering events lady muttering about us all being 'gay' left us in no doubt we were a tremendous disappointment to the local economy!

It wasn't unusual for my hosts in various cities to suggest visiting local 'tourist attractions', I say that loosely. At that time Russia didn't encourage tourism and the places were seldom attractive. However, it was often more interesting checking out their thoughtful recommendations rather than spending the afternoon in a dreary hotel room.

This is what led me to the Central Siberian Geological Museum, which contained an incredible range of rare semi-precious stones found only in the Urals.

The museum was really very impressive. A lot of money had been invested to display the vast array of semi-precious stones, mainly in secure glass cabinets.

I was offered the only English-speaking guide, a lady of mature age who had a particularly domineering way about her. She was evidently more used to school parties than providing solo British businessmen with information on her specialist subject. This was typical of what I'd seen within the Russian school and museum system.

As the only member of her 'tour party' the small baton aloft she carried seemed unnecessary, and it wasn't long before I found out what it was for. She led me through the museum as though marching at the head of a crocodile of small unruly boys. Each time she stopped in front of a display she would rap sharply on the glass with her baton and exclaim "pay attention".

After the fourth or fifth time, as she raised her hand to strike, I said quietly "I am paying attention". She looked at me with the disdain of Medusa, despite my being the only other person in the entire museum, and proceeded to tap three times on the next cabinet before repeating her catch phrase once again. I promise I tried not to giggle, although she pushed me to my limit. The museum was excellent though, definitely worth a visit next time you're in Siberia.

Towards the end of the week the Kodak team planned a barbeque on the banks of the river Ob, the seventh biggest waterway in the world, which flows through Novosibirsk. The location just outside the city was on a picturesque bend in the river. The evening was perfect, the sinking light and summer warmth meant everything was set for an enjoyable relaxed session with the trainees.

Except it wasn't! Out of nowhere a deep black swarm of mosquitoes descended on us in malevolent formation. Retreating to the smoke zone of the barbeque and downing numerous beers as a chemical weapon against mozzie attack seemed like a good idea. Wrong again! Waking up in a painful haze the following morning I was covered in the worst mosquito bites I've experienced anywhere in the world.

The Kodak team in Novosibirsk did all they could to make the visit memorable, and the week I spent in the city stood out as one of the more interesting excursions into deepest Russia. It turns out that once you make a friend in Russia, you have a friend for life!

Sometime later, on a brief visit to Kodak's UK site at Hemel Hempstead I was walking down the concourse when two hosts from the Novosibirsk event appeared beside me. Their booming voices ringing and echoing through the building. "Hey Mike, it's great to see you."

Now these guys were big burly men, but I was no minnow, standing over 6' and weighing in at 14 stone. Nevertheless, to the bewilderment and consternation of the Kodak employees milling around, I was swept up in a bear hug and spun round like a rag doll.

A Russian friend is a friend indeed.

PART III

Behind The Red Curtain

Chapter Twenty-Eight :

Back in the USSR

Kodak's global growth had seen massive inroads into the USSR and where Kodak had staff, I inevitably followed to train them. The top man was Tom Garman, a general manager from the American arm of the company who was overseeing Kodak's spread into a Russia desperate to welcome in western investment.

Tom had a proposition for me. Would I consider including candidates from Rosinter in my training and live part-time in Russia to smooth the process? Rosinter was a joint venture company working in tandem with Kodak, and many of the stores up and running under Kodak branding were actually franchises owned by Rosinter.

To ensure great customer service and staff retention across the brand, my behavioral management training was going to be essential for both the Kodak team and the franchise staff.

It seems I made quite an impact on the Rosinter CEO, Rostislav Ordovsky-Taneavsky-Blanco, the son of a Russian émigré and a Spaniard who had been born in Venezuela and was now making the most of the goldmine the opening of the USSR offered to the global market.

Rosistlav was debonaire, articulate and charismatic. With a hint of his exotic ancestry, his hair and beard, obviously inherited from his father's DNA, was a shade somewhere between milk chocolate and dirty blond and it shone when it caught the light. He had an easy smile and affable manner, but you certainly didn't cross him. Rostislav already had a reputation as a fine businessman, even within the confines of Kodak. I had vast admiration for all he had already accomplished in Russia since moving there from Venezuela aged just 25.

"If you ever need a job, I want you to talk to me first" he said in his smooth, mid-Atlantic accent at the end of our first meeting.

Those words came to the forefront of my mind on my return to Kodak. Rumours of impending redundancies had been in the wind for a while. The company had become over-staffed at a time when reliance on film and photo-processing stores was reducing with the advent of digital cameras.

Now each department was expected to meet targets for redundancies. No job was safe, but with that perspective came opportunity.

At that time in the HR training team there were just two of us achieving our targets for the business, a chap named Trevor Horne and me. The boss had been given instructions to cull staff numbers and the writing was on the wall for several colleagues. Trevor and I weren't blind to the increasingly bleak future of Kodak and like me, he had feelers out for a new role and had already agreed a consultancy post as a side hustle. To the astonishment and relief of our colleagues, both Trevor and I offered to take redundancy, much to the surprise of the management.

Whilst it was a significant shock to him, the boss, a manager of the old school interested only in numbers and logistics, thought we were teaching psychobabble. It might have been construed as essential to the business but to him NLP and behavioural training was hogwash. He was glad to be rid of us and happy to have achieved his redundancy targets so efficiently, although perhaps he didn't consider the ultimate impact on his team of losing his two best members of staff – but that was no skin off my nose.

I called Rostislav and offered my services immediately my redundancy was finalised. And so it was, on Maundy Thursday 1998 I walked away from Kodak and flew to Moscow to begin my new role with Rosinter, a retail and hospitality giant making its mark on the USSR. The initial reason for my recruitment was for me to take on responsibility for training and mentoring photographic staff based in Kodak franchises owned by Rosinter in and around Moscow. As it turned out, that was just the beginning, and any preconceptions I had about my new role were soon to be shattered.

Chapter Twenty-Nine :

Driving in Moscow

It was clear I'd need to travel all over Moscow on a regular basis and would require a car and driver. Dima, a slight, nervous Russian boy of 20 was recruited to assist me. Evidently this was his first proper job, and although awkward about working with someone he could not understand, he was happy to spend his days driving me out to distant suburbs. Despite the significant age difference, we quickly became a great working duo.

These were early days and my Russian language skills were pretty much non-existent. Dima spoke no English which made every day more complicated. After a while we found a selection of words we could use and developed our own patois which would have baffled everyone else.

The 'company car' was a white Lada7 and in a pretty bad state of repair. Road safety and comfort were alien concepts on the Moscow streets. The worst aspect as a chauffeured passenger was the two-inch gap between the seat and back rest, leaving it open to the howling winter wind blasting the nether regions. The short-term solution was an impromptu draught excluder made of the nice warm Russian coat I so desperately needed in a vehicle devoid of heating.

The car was somewhat unreliable. When it first broke down at -18 degrees Dima got out to look under the bonnet to establish what was wrong. I also got out and he made it clear that whilst a manly Russian could bear the cold, a soft foreigner should remain in the car.

On behalf of every Englishman, I stood my ground. The subject was never raised again and on the many occasions the Lada let us down, I was shoulder to shoulder with Dima until it was back on the road.

My first and only company car – the infamous Lada

The car had a registration plate with red lettering on a white background to indicate it was foreign owned. This gave carte blanche for zealous police officers to stop us for a range of apparent traffic offences whenever it suited them. It was never clear what the offence was, but the resultant penalty was always a fine in US dollars, handed over on the spot with no paperwork to back up the charges.

Another expat was stopped six times in one day which he subsequently claimed as an ironic world record. Doing business in Moscow in the 1990s was very lucrative … primarily for the traffic police.

Apart from the centre of the city, the rest of Moscow was drab and gloomy. Grey buildings and virtually no street lighting made it a dark, foreboding place. No wonder vodka consumption was so high.

Escaping the city by day was like travelling back in time. Fields were ploughed by farm horses, and we were regularly held up by carts drawn by rake-thin nags which no doubt worked until they dropped. Roads became dirt tracks, lined by wooden huts with smoke drifting in a hazy fug from the rickety chimney stacks. Old ladies would sit outside on stools, sewing and crafting to sell or decorate their homes. The vegetable plots beside every dwelling were clearly a necessity rather than a hobby, but they gave locals something their city-neighbours could only enjoy if they happened to have an allotment – fresh food!

Many poorer city dwellers seemed to have an allotment at the far end of a metro line. With cheap travel the mini gardens offered a day out in the country and a significant boost to the meagre supplies available in the supermarkets. They would spend Sunday on the allotment and return with produce which was stacked in the communal corridors of apartment buildings – you'd have to squeeze past it to reach the lift. Despite the challenges of life in Moscow, I don't think the produce ever got taken by neighbours. It was sacrosanct.

But I digress. After a few months it was decided I was competent to drive around Moscow without a driver, so goodbye Dima.

Actually, this was much more daunting than it might sound. This was pre-satnav and without road maps and barely able to decipher the Cyrillic street signs, I would often stop to try and work out where I was. Even if I asked a passerby, I usually didn't understand their reply.

When the roads were really bad, Dima had made a habit of driving through the parks to get to wherever we needed to go. Once I took my place behind the wheel I did the same thing, scattering pedestrians as I drove through the city parks to reach my destination and avoid the clanking traffic jams in the city centre.

Dima and I had spent many a happy hour cruising around trying to find our destinations, so over time I had built up a pretty good mental picture of many parts of the city. This was borne out on the occasions when I needed to take Russians out with me on my travels. They were amazed I knew where to drive to – most couldn't even conceive of owning a car and went only as far as the Metro would take them.

Working away from home was taking a toll, and Rostislav was more than aware of the challenges for Leila and me, while I was spending 6 – 8 weeks in Moscow at a time. I was only popping back for an occasional weekend. He understood our relationship was very important to me and suggested the company pay for Leila to fly to Moscow and spend the weekend with me in the city.

As Leila was a first timer to the city, we did all of the regular tourist stuff, driving to Red Square, the Kremlin, Sparrow Hills, the Luzhniki Stadium and we spent the evenings wining and dining at high end Rosinter restaurants.

Leila had a ball, travelling around the city seeing all the best bits, but what she didn't realise was we only did the safe areas, steadfastly avoiding the dodgy parts of the city which were part of my daily life. She was oblivious to the two-man armed security detail tailing us everywhere we went and had no concept of the real risk to life that an expat living in the centre of the city took.

Ultimately Rosinter's security team decided I had been in the city long enough to know the area and drive myself around without assistance. Dima had taught me well. Each time I reached the car, aside from clearing ice from the windows, I checked underneath for tracking devices. You never knew who was watching or who might have taken umbrage at my presence, or perhaps saw me as a potentially lucrative kidnapping target. This became a habit and for years afterwards any car I drove would be carefully examined before I got in.

One Saturday night I went to a social event outside the Moscow ring road, the MKAD. It's the equivalent of the M25 but unlike driving over the London orbital road, a return crossing of the MKAD after dark meant a mandatory vehicle check. There was virtually no traffic when I was stopped on a bleak roundabout above the road. I had personal papers with me, you never went anywhere in Russia without your documents, but nothing for the car. The company had neglected to tell me they were tucked behind the visor.

I was escorted to a large dark green vehicle which looked as though it would have been more at home out on the tundra. This was a new and unnerving experience, and I had no idea what was going on. It turned out this was a breath test – but this wasn't a 'blow in the bag' job. No, they required a full blood sample, inexpertly drawn by a squat babushka in a lab-coat.

As the guards stood eagerly by the door anticipating a positive result and a payday from nailing the 'foreigner', the woman analyzed the sample for what seemed like forever. I sat there sweating, knowing I could end up in jail. Eventually, much to the annoyance of my captors, she looked up and said "nyet."

Thankfully this was the one night I'd had nothing to drink. The door opened and I returned to the car, aware of my lucky escape. The relief didn't kick in until I was safely home.

Chapter Thirty :

Interpreters

I definitely needed an interpreter, although even this basic interaction was something of a minefield.

The first one, Sasha, was a pretty, petite 18-year-old whose parents insisted on meeting me to extract a promise I would not violate their daughter. This wasn't an issue, as mixing work with pleasure wasn't on my agenda.

I can't imagine any Edwardian suitor would have been grilled more thoroughly. That being said, I understood their concern and might well have done the same had I been in their position. International businessmen were notorious for abusing their position with subordinate female staff and they'd given us all a bad name.

However, I don't think the girl got the 'no fraternization' memo. Although she sat demurely through the parental interview, her perspective on our business arrangement would have made her father's copious nostril hair curl. Sasha believed I was her route to the West.

Sitting in the back of the unreliable Lada, Sasha would press close, thigh snuggled against mine as I inched my way towards the door. This in itself was risky. The door opened with the slightest pressure and tumbling out onto a Moscow street wasn't high on my list of enjoyable things to do. After a couple of days, Dima, responding to my evident discomfort, came up with a solution. As I walked out to the car he stood to attention and opened the front passenger door. I gratefully slipped in and took my place as 'shotgun' – to a torrent of angry recriminations.

There were lots of perks to being an interpreter in soviet Russia. I always ate in decent company restaurants and once the opportunity to get up close and personal in the car had been taken away, Sasha lost no time in suggesting she should join me for meals so I could chat with other businessmen.

In theory this was a great idea. Mealtimes could be lonely affairs so with Sasha's assistance I opened conversations with individuals or groups of diners. This started well, and by asking general questions I was learning more about business in the city and growing my network. However, it gradually dawned on me from the awkward responses of my companions, that far from translating my words, Sasha was in fact laying down the law on my behalf.

The chill in the air had nothing to do with the temperature and the one thing I didn't want to do was rile my new connections. Sasha found herself unemployed and was replaced by a new model. Sveta was an avid feminist who announced at interview there would be 'no sex'. That was fine with me.

However, even with this ardent feminist on my team, there were bizarre moments. As I prepared for one of my regular return visits to the UK, she announced she was unhappy with the quality of her underwear, and insisted I must purchase attractive lingerie from Marks and Spencer to bring back for her. I explained to Sveta that my wife would take a dim view of this 'innocent transaction' and if she saw me packing scanties for another woman it would send her into a rage.

Interpreters came and went. Each had their quirks, and that made it all the more fun.

Chapter Thirty-One :

Day trip to Obninsk 1998

After my move to Rosinter, I found myself on a politically sensitive secondment to Kodak Russia with a number of disparate responsibilities. One of these was to manage seven Kodak Express shops in and around Moscow.

The primary aim was to help the staff with interpersonal skills which it's fair to say were somewhat lacking, so in the main I ran training programmes in the head office and staff came to me.

However, being a dutiful manager, I wanted to see my teams at work in their regular environment. Some of the shops were relatively central, but others were way out in the suburbs.

Initially I would travel with my driver and interpreter, and we gradually worked our way around the stores, improving the way each worked and seeing the staff benefit from the change in perspective to a more 'customer service' point of view.

After a while it occurred to me, we had made regular visits to just six of the seven stores on my books. For some reason the seventh never made it onto my calendar. Asking my colleagues in head office to explain, it transpired the missing store was in Obninsk, some 100km outside Moscow but no one ever went there… Interesting!

My curiosity peaked, I decided to go and check it out. Always up for an adventure, my driver Dima along with Sveta, my current translator, piled into the old Lada with me and headed southwest.

Sveta was something of an enigma, tall with a muscular build, self-assured and a tough, no-nonsense attitude. Her physical and mental strength and attention to every detail made me wonder whether she had been in the military, or perhaps was still employed by Russian intelligence to watch my every move. Her scruffy appearance and wild short brown hair were a good disguise if that was the case. Was I not worthy of someone more like Xenia Onatopp than Rosa Klebb?

At one point, in a bid to escape what she described as her 'terrible accommodation' Sveta pitched moving into the spare bedroom of the luxurious Park Place apartment I had managed to secure thanks to my Kodak connections. She proposed to cook, clean, make herself generally indispensable, and increase the number and intensity of our Russian lessons. Trying to mask the fear in my eyes, I turned her down. I'm not entirely convinced the landlord's decision to evict me from that finely appointed residence a couple of days later was entirely unconnected, but hey ho. A man with a wife is best off avoiding any potential honey-trap, even if the honey has already been eaten by a slightly musky female bear.

But I digress, back en route to Obninsk Dima drove along a virtually empty dual carriageway and followed the signs off the main route to a much smaller road. Immediately after the junction we came upon a red and white sentry box and barrier, very much like a customs post or border control, but we were just 70 miles from Moscow and over 700 miles from the nearest border. There was no sign of any guards, and the barrier was up, so without thinking about it, we drove straight through.

Unbeknown to any of us, this had been, until very recently, a closed town of 100,000 residents. Its purpose, apparently, was the development of nuclear energy for peaceful purposes - well, that's the story they told me. Read up on it and see what you think!

You needed passes to get in and passes to leave. Understandably, very few people left.

Obninsk was unusual in that it had good amenities, and every home had a telephone line which was unheard of at that time – but then I suppose the authorities wanted to be sure they heard every discussion which happened in those homes!

The workers and their families were segregated completely from the rest of Russia, and yet I had driven straight in. These people rarely saw other Russians, and although it transpired the restrictions had been lifted just days earlier thanks to an intervention by Mikael Gorbachev, the community was beyond surprised to find a foreigner in their midst.

I was carefully observed, and groups of people gathered to take a closer look at the tall, bearded stranger as the three of us found a restaurant and took pleasure in a lunch of significantly better quality than routinely available in other towns and cities.

We had a pleasant and interesting day visiting the Kodak Express and had a look around the town. It seemed rude not to check out this mysterious place before we drove back to the relative freedom of Moscow.

That evening I met expat and Russian friends for supper and told them of my impromptu visit to Obninsk. They were disbelieving, mocking me, and suggesting I'd got it wrong. "This is impossible Mike, Obninsk is closed, out of bounds, maybe it doesn't even exist".

It took describing the journey, the town, the vast power plant and the empty sentry point in detail, along with several bottles of vodka, before my companions were convinced an Englishman had made it unhindered and unnoticed to the centre of the Soviet Union's nuclear technology and research.

Chapter Thirty-Two :

Moscow Life

Whilst working for Rosinter I was kicking my heels at the weekend and was frankly bored. Rostislav had an inner circle of Venezuelan pals around him. They didn't seem to do any work or have much purpose other than to be part of the scenery in the clubs and restaurants. I never saw them serve as bodyguards, because that would have marked him out for greater attention from the FSB. Instead Rostislav had Russian security. Perhaps Venezuelans came and went, learning on the job before opening new businesses in other countries for Rosinter. I never took much notice of them, although I knew they were aware of me. It seemed Rostislav regarded me as a significant player in his organisation, and I had open access to the boss, while others, including the clique of his countrymen, had to make an appointment.

Rostislav suggested I might like to take an interest in another arm of the business, the hospitality sector, which until then I knew almost nothing about.

I spent a lot of time touring restaurants supposedly helping the managers do a better job, but in reality, I was overseeing the operation and keeping a close eye on team management. Rosinter's reach covered everything from a Kentucky type take-out, pizza and pasta to fine dining restaurants and the franchise for TGI Friday. It was a really big operation, in a time when this just wasn't happening in Moscow. The clientele was primarily Russian and a few party-going expats. The turnover would have been around $50 million when a Muscovite middle manager might have been clearing $1000 a month and thought he was wealthy.

Expat in Moscow

My priority was the high end of the operation covering a variety of international restaurants and clubs across the city. I spent a lot of time in the Santa Fe, and anyone who knows Moscow will know the place. Unsurprisingly it's a large Tex-Mex restaurant with around 150 seats located on the ground floor and on the upper floor you'd find a boutique Japanese restaurant, also part of the Rosinter group.

In the basement was a nightclub called Hippopotam which had a security arch to scan clients for their guns, knives, and other weapons. It was a well-known haunt for prostitutes and mafia.

Javier was a senior manager at the complex. A vivacious New Yorker in his early thirties, he was proud of his culture and South American lineage. I can't recall whether his roots were from the Inca or Mayan civilization, but it didn't matter, he felt at home wherever he was. Although he was compact, his slight physique and boundless energy gave the impression he was always in motion. Javier possessed a warm and undeniable charm which captivated those around him.

Javier's most striking feature was his infectious smile, a big, welcoming grin which lit up his olive face and crinkled his eyes all the way to his sideburns and thatch of jet-black hair. His friendly nature drew people in effortlessly and put everyone at ease. He had thrown himself into his new Russian lifestyle, married a gorgeous girl from a suburb of the city, and they had just welcomed a new baby. He had become an important part of the Rosinter set up and a close, and valued buddy of mine.

On one fateful night while I was away in the UK, his driver dropped him at the entrance to his building just about 3am. Javier's wife heard the car stop and her husband say goodnight as he closed the car door, but he never made it up the stairs to his home.

Despite enquiries and frantic searches, we never found out who snatched him from the street or what happened to him, but on my return from leave I was interrogated by the Rosinter head of security, an ex-KGB colonel with close ties to the FSB, the Russian secret police.

The Hollywood version of a Russian cross examination in all its harsh malevolence wasn't far from the truth. Although I wasn't in a police station or secret HQ, I might as well have been.

The colonel sat there, shoulders wide in braided uniform looking as though he'd just marched in from the May-Day parade, ready to intimidate. The muscles in his face did not respond to either his questions or my answers. He might have been set in stone, staring at me, eyeball to eyeball with a hot bright light glaring into my face, burning my eyes.

As the translator at his side barked his questions, he threw photos across the table, "Do you know this girl, what about this one?" A case was being built, not to find Javier, but to justify his disappearance.

I remembered being reassured in my early days with Rosinter that any misdemeanor committed by staff in the city from drink-driving to murder would be smoothed out, alibis provided where necessary and even the most heinous crime would fade away. I guess that worked both ways.

The story they cooked up suggested Javier had been leading a double life, with two passports and a stable of women. The final conclusion, reached and accepted by the company, was that he had gone to the airport at 3.30am and flown out of the country with a girlfriend – never to be seen again.

The fact that flights didn't take off from the city airport until late afternoon was completely irrelevant. The gaping holes in the cover-up reinforced the belief that Javier was a victim of a plot, either state sanctioned or because he had offended one of the many mafiosi in the city.

Javier's sister was a New York cop and came to Moscow to investigate. Sadly, she got nowhere. The city doesn't reveal its secrets, but then neither did a multinational company.

On one night I was in the Santa Fe and left around midnight in my beat-up Lada 7, the only car in the carpark which wasn't a large SUV with blacked out windows. Despite that, one vehicle stood out – a Mercedes - the mafia like to be sure you've noticed them.

Minutes after I drove off, a man who had followed me out of the club, along with his driver, were assassinated. Fascinatingly, within moments, OMON, the special forces turned up and sealed off the area. They'd clearly known the hit was about to go down and cleared all the Santa-Fe security out of the building. No one was ever arrested or charged, and I never 'officially' heard what it was all about. Just another night in Moscow!

I tended to keep a low profile as best I could, but one night driving back from Santa- Fe I was pretty sure I was being followed. I pulled my car into the apartment parking, still aware of the car tailing me. I went up to my apartment, put the lights on, then looked down to see what was going on. Rookie mistake. I watched the occupants slip down in their seats trying to be invisible. I'd played right into their hands and shown them exactly where I lived.

I learned my lesson. From that point on I would always leave a light on in the apartment, and on arrival at the building, ride the lift to an upper floor and sneak back down on the stairs, letting myself in to an apartment which, from the outside, looked as though it had been occupied all evening.

The uncomfortable combination of constant surveillance and a desire for a decent lifestyle meant living in Moscow wasn't as straightforward as choosing an apartment and staying long term. There was constant pressure to relocate because the places were just awful. The allowance paid by Rosinter for accommodation didn't go far, and the buildings were so decrepit they really should have been condemned.

I thought I'd got lucky when the opportunity arose to rent a one-bedroom apartment 15 minutes from central Moscow by metro. The place was in great condition, perhaps slightly feminine, but I could live with that.

Everything was going swimmingly until the translator explained the landlady, a statuesque, bosomy blonde, was moving out to spend more time in her home city of Samara, around 1000km from Moscow. She would return each month to oversee her business in the capital. "Where does she stay when she comes back" I asked naively. "Well here with you of course" was the all too clear response. Needless to say, I left and didn't go back. It was just another example of the way Russian women were incredibly liberated in their attitude to exchanging sex for opportunity.

Such was the life of an expat in Moscow.

On a bitterly cold winter day, while Dima was still driving me around and Sasha was working as my interpreter, we were en route to Rosinter sites and drove around a bend next to a construction site. On the pavement was a man, flat out with smoke coming out of his sleeves and trouser legs. Three or four guys were just standing there looking at him. I assumed he had been massively electrocuted. I exclaimed to Dima and Sasha that we should do something to help but they were totally disinterested. In Moscow it seemed sights like this were best ignored. If it's nothing to do with them, they stay out of it and say nothing. I rather suspect that would be the case in any communist or autocratic state. Keep your mouth and eyes shut, don't criticize, don't get involved and never do anything to rock the boat.

*

One of the perks of being in Moscow was dining in the best restaurants without having to pay and having access to live music whenever it suited me.

I saw a 72-year-old Chuck Berry leaping around the stage at the Luzhniki Stadium in 1998 and was offered backstage passes for the Rolling Stones although for some reason I didn't bother going to meet them after the show. The CEO of Rosinter had a lot of local influence and opened many doors for his staff.

Chapter Thirty-Three :

Bolshoi

My fellow Brit, Michael Bedford, was a big, exuberant man whose loud voice and short back and sides, combined with Savile Row grooming, gave him the patina of the British establishment, or at least alumni status from one of the better private schools. Contrary to appearances this wasn't the case. Michael came from humble beginnings, and had worked his mensa-level intelligence hard to improve his status. Now divorced from his first wife and highly regarded as a business consultant, he had been brought in to guide Rosinter through a new project and was spending a lot of time at the office. Out of hours we were quietly considering teaming up to bring a Starbucks franchise to Moscow.

Michael and I habitually took the opportunity to socialize together. Having another native English speaker who understood my humour and references eased some of the weight of long periods of time away from Leila.

We would occasionally foray into the local bars rather than those reserved for expats. Here we could have a couple of drinks without being hassled by ladies of the night. The only slight fly in the ointment was that these were mostly Mafia haunts and the sight of two stylish Englishmen was enough to silence the room.

Thanks to our respective translators, we'd each learned to speak enough Russian with what would have been a laughable English accent, to order vodka on repeat. From experience we found the best way to reassure a suspicious henchman was to get quickly and quietly drunk. Most of the time after the Mafioso's curiosity had worn off, they became very friendly and the drinks and illuminating conversation would flow long after the capacity for lucid speech was forgotten.

It was only after spending some 'quality time' in one such bar that Michael and I ditched the Starbucks idea. We'd picked up enough back-channel information to realise such a small-scale operation would be no match for the Russian mafia. I guess you could say doing our unique form of due diligence helped us reach the conclusion we would rather be alive than dead.

Working late one evening in the Rosinter office with Michael, who was now acting Vice-President of Rosinter, the larger-than-life Rostislav materialized beside us, enthusiastically waving tickets which were no longer required by a corporate hospitality guest.

Rostislav wanted us to go to the Bolshoi Ballet that night. The VIP tickets were expensive, and it would be a shame to waste them. The only thing was, we'd have to leave now, as the ballet was about to start.

If you look on a route-planning app, it will tell you it's a twenty-five-minute drive to do the 8.9km from the Rosinter office to the Bolshoi Theatre. We made it in fifteen, but even so the curtain had gone up on the night's performance of Giselle.

Now the Russians take their ballet very seriously. The Bolshoi is the crème de la crème of artistic endeavour. Understandably, having arrived late, we anticipated waiting for the interval before going to our seats. In any case, Michael and I were ready for a drink, having been ripped away from our meeting without a moment's notice.

But no, on checking our tickets the theatre ushers were most insistent on taking us straight to our seats … up a flight of stairs and along the edge of the auditorium …

Anger rippled through the audience in the stalls and on the balcony, at the interruption by two burly blokes being hustled past the seats of culturally charged Muscovites already enjoying their art.

To add insult to the impact of our arrival, it turned out the VIP seats in question were, in fact, a grand box just 5 metres above the right-hand side of the stage. Opening the door, the usherette discovered it had been colonized by four Russians who, the performance having started, had snuck in for a free upgrade.

Much ill-tempered whispering saw the interlopers evicted. By now the audience were totally mesmerized by the antics, and even the dancers' confused faces turned to the commotion just above their heads.

The performance now thoroughly disrupted; we brazened it out despite the murmuring below us. Come the interval, it was Michael who braved the black looks and tutting when he went for the obligatory vodka and returned with a bottle to numb the embarrassment.

As the curtain fell after the final curtain call, we turned up our coat collars and left quickly, unwilling to engage the wrath of the aficionados for whom Giselle might never be the same again.

Chapter Thirty-Four :

Katya and Irina 1997

Joachim had parted company with his first wife, and ten years to the day after joining Kodak, had received an enticing offer from cigarette conglomerate Philip Morris which was impossible to reject. To my delight, he relocated to Moscow. Batman and Robin were together again.

Joachim moved into a tiny studio apartment located on Michurinskiy Prospekt which was only a stone's throw from the Kodak offices where I was based. We spent a lot of time together after work, filling the hours hanging out in various clubs and bars. Long periods working in Russia had drawn us into communities of Kodak employees and expats, and we had many friends in common, including one who, unbeknown to me, had made quite an impact on my favourite German co-conspirator!

When Joachim started working at Philip Morris, he was surprised to run into a friendly face, a young woman named Katya, who had coincidentally also started working for the company.

Now Katya had been a receptionist at the Kodak Mosfilm Studio while she studied English at the university's night school. She had caught Joachim's eye and he often connected with her while he was planning his trips to the various Russian companies he was contracted to work with.

Katya

One of the venues I had easy access to via my increasing circle of contacts was the ultra-glamourous Kodak Kin Mir, a single screen 570 seat cinema which offered the first modern entertainment facilities in Russia. It was in the centre of the city in a building on Tverskaya Street, which had once been the home of the Izvestia Newspaper, the mouthpiece of the defunct Soviet government.

The blockbuster movie that summer was 'Titanic'. I managed to get hold of three tickets, and casually mentioned there was a spare if Joachim wanted to bring someone along. It never crossed my mind that he would do so! It turned out Joachim liked Katya a lot and had been looking for an 'in' she would find irresistible. The opportunity to go to the cinema was quite a coup in Moscow at that time, so Joachim invited Katya to spend an evening at the Kin Mir, along with his 'best friend Mike', she didn't hesitate because she remembered me as a 'true gentleman' from her Kodak days. So off we went, three of us on their 'first date'!

Katya sat between the two of us, and when the film came to its inevitable conclusion with (spoiler alert) Leonardo DiCaprio sinking to the depths of the ice cold north Atlantic ocean, to Katya's embarrassment, the only sound was of muted sobs and spluttering from her elderly companions, one more elderly than the other, as Joachim would ask me to point out! The two of us were in pieces, snot mingling with tears and cascading unappealingly down our chins. We were barely able to look at one another for fear of more heart-wrenching blubbing ripping from our manly chests. Katya for her part was less impressed by the Hollywood tearjerker, which barely touched her deep Russian soul!

Far from giving them a sinking feeling, Titanic was the beginning of a fine romance for Joachim and Katya. They made a great couple, and to my joy our friendship continued unabated.

For years Joachim and I had spent a lot of our free time together and now Katya was on the scene, he saw no need to change his routine, but in reality it was awkward going to restaurants and clubs as a threesome, so unbeknown to me, Katya hit on a solution.

Joachim and Katya

Enter Irina, Katya's best friend and the woman she had decided I should marry, regardless of the presence of Leila in my life. Yes, you read that correctly. Katya and Irina each wanted wedding bells and their 'happy-ever-after', and set out to make it happen, with very little consideration for the opinion of their proposed grooms!

Katya was so used to me being around in Moscow, she gave no thought to my life back in England. For my part, I loved Leila and had no intention of doing anything to mess up our relationship.

There's no question it was more convenient to go out as a foursome, but having been warned of the plot by Joachim, I was studiously ignoring the obvious overtures. I think they were all surprised I didn't take things further, but there was never any question in my mind.

Irina was charming, intelligent, great fun to be around, and determined to remain celibate until she was wed. That was no problem. Lovely as she was, I had no intention of falling into a Russian rom-com escapade.

However, the girls were determined. I was taken to meet Irina's parents who felt their daughter had scored a winner. It didn't seem to matter that I was a generation older than they were, and thirty years older than Irina. Here was an Englishman who would change their daughter's fortunes, provide stability and take care of her, as all good businessmen do with their Russian wives.

At this time, I was running a high-end club and several restaurants for Rosinter, as well as overseeing a chain of takeaways. Each night I would spot-check them, always at different times, to ensure they were meeting the standards the company expected.

Simultaneously I was being seen as a target for husband-hungry Russian girls who had got used to seeing me coming in and out of the establishments. They were becoming a nuisance.

Irina proved the ideal solution. She loved to dress up and enjoyed fine dining, so rather than make my visits alone, she would come along as my companion. We got on well, and although she still had her long-term goal in mind (and made sure I knew it) she was a splendid deterrent to unwelcome attention.

The only problem was that my expat colleagues jumped to the conclusion that this attractive young thing was more than a friend. To be fair, her outfits left nothing to the imagination, but with a body like that, who could blame her? I would see the smiles, raised eyebrows and conclusions being jumped to. It wasn't comfortable, but spending time with Irina solved more problems than it caused. I could go home to Leila with a clear conscience and know I had made a friend for life.

Chapter Thirty-Five :

May Day in Moscow

I was staying in an apartment in Kitai Gorod, which is Russian for 'China Town.' Despite my expectations of regular Chinese food and sense of community, I was to be disappointed. The Chinese had moved out many decades before, just leaving the name and an aura of faded grandeur. This part of Moscow strongly resembles baroque Rome, or perhaps Paris with tall 'palazzo' type buildings that were once the residences of successful merchants who would have traded the globe. Those beautiful buildings had now been divided into apartments, and one was to become my home for just a few months… it wasn't wise to stay for longer than that. Expats were encouraged to change location frequently for their own security.

The apartment was large in proportion, but eerily dark and gloomy. Despite the large windows, it never really seemed light or welcoming. During the night I could hear the cockroaches scrabbling across the wooden floor; the noise of insects wearing steel capped boots woke me regularly. Turn on a lamp and they would disappear, only to resume their nocturnal marching when darkness returned.

Despite regular fumigation, these resilient insects made maximum use of the internal ducting system as a route throughout the building. No apartment was inaccessible to them and moving any piece of furniture would result in a scattering of shiny black bodies to the nearest crack or crevice.

But being in the heart of Old Moscow did have some perks. It was an architecturally beautiful location and only a five-minute walk along empty roads to the famous GUM store, the most elegant department store in all Russia, with its famous arched roof and parallel galleries. At that time, it was primarily selling ex-soviet memorabilia, army surplus, Russian dolls and, of course, Vodka.

I'd walk down an alley at the side of the GUM out into Red Square. In Moscow the arrival of spring is a longed-for end to the bitter winter months, and as April tipped into May, wandering through Kitai Gorod on a sunny Sunday was almost like being in southern Europe.

The May Parade was the greatest opportunity for the Government of the Soviet Union to show off its military might – an occasion for the West to observe hardware, missiles and armies in awe.

But earlier in May the square was empty, it was just me and a couple of young servicemen at the entrance to the Kremlin. On any other year I'd never have made it past armed police and security personnel; I'd have likely been bundled into a van and interrogated, presumed a spy and potentially, like one of my friends, found lifeless. The FSB used Lubyanka prison for such assessments. It was famous for inmates 'accidentally' falling from its high windows and healthy detainees experiencing heart attacks.

Not this time however. By 1998 Boris Yeltsin was overseeing the dismantling of the old Soviet Union, and along with his more liberal views, friendship was the message the Russians wanted to convey to allies in the West.

Like so many times in my life and travels, I happened to be in a place where I could see and enjoy a different perspective. Observing Red Square without the cacophony of the Russian army that spring day gave me hope. The return of the Military Parade under President Vladimir Putin in 2014 was a herald of darker days ahead.

Chapter Thirty-Six :

Nizhny Novgorod - Ekranoplan

Olga worked in the training department at Rosinter and could speak English. She was petite, stocky and habitually wore a pale green trench coat which really suited her coppery red hair. Single by choice and liberated in attitude, she didn't take nonsense from me or anyone else and it took her a while to see the funny side of my very British sense of humour. Olga originally provided a service as my translator, and gradually became a co-presenter and we ran training programmes together.

Olga (green coat) my translator and co-presenter

On our journeys together to other parts of Russia, often by train or plane, she would talk to me about Russian history as she knew it. She described the old days, pre-Glasnost, the time of the Cold War when everyone lived on their nerves.

The long uninspiring camouflage green overnight trains resembled the Orient Express, but in a shabby faded way no starlet or millionaire would choose. The trains were serviceable, but old and despite the attendant on duty in every car, the passenger was vulnerable. For safety, and in all likelihood to save some roubles for Rosinter, we would share a cabin on the long overnight journeys, reinforcing the lock with a champagne cork, taken along for the purpose of preventing the decrepit door from being opened from the outside while we slept.

Olga would bring food and vodka for the journey and often talked of the military hardware of which the USSR had been so proud, showing it off in vast parades and intimidating 'almost but not quite' threats to the West.

On the night train to Nizhny Novogrod, a city just to the west of the Caucasus region, Olga told me of a sea skimming bomber, the 'Ekranoplan' which terrified the Americans and had the potential to devastate the eastern (and probably western) seaboard of the States. Two were built, one stayed in the harbour on the Black Sea, but the other was in the very city we were travelling to. Would I like to see it?

It never crossed my mind this fearsome warmongering machine might be abandoned on a site we drove past every morning traveling to the training location. The area was just like any other industrial estate, but even more grey, dusty and dismal. It really matched the weather and our mood.

Pulling up in the car, the driver displaying zero interest in our peculiar behaviour, we peered through the windows of an empty decaying building and there it was!

Anybody could have found it, even taken it away almost unnoticed, but then I remembered that nothing goes unseen in Russia. But why was it there, easily visible but left to rot in the back end of the sixth largest city in the USSR?

I suppose with the dawn of the new, more open Russia which came in the 1990s, the Government had no need of sabre-rattling and military force. The tools of the cold war were put on ice – permanently.

Chapter Thirty-Seven :

Kiev

Working for Rosinter took me all over the USSR and flying into Kiev in the Crimea was seldom without incident.

On one occasion I'd arrived in the early evening and checked into my hotel, yet another homage to Stalinist architecture.

All over Russia the hotels I stayed in looked identical. They were state run, and from Minsk to Almaty in what is now Kazakhstan, they were large, foreboding and had the same dull camouflage green décor throughout. The receptionists were, to a woman, as grey and unfriendly as their surroundings. Guests were barely tolerated, but once ensconced there was an expectation one would make use of the generous supply of local prostitutes plying their wares and no doubt paying the staff a commission in cash or in kind.

I checked in and went to my spartan room. There was nothing to speak of aside from a bed and nightstand. The luxury of anything else, even something as simple as a means to make a coffee, was many years into the future and most restaurants closed by 6pm. The one thing which did work was the phone. The first call came within minutes of my arrival – would I like a woman sent up?

I said no thank you and settled down to prepare for the next day's course. Thirty minutes later the phone rang again "we have beautiful women to choose from, would you like to see one?" Another negative answer before the third call came in "can we send you a boy instead?"

I gave them ten out of ten for tenacity, and eventually they accepted my polite refusals, but the currency of prostitution, along with the unwelcome cockroach room companions, were part of life travelling in the USSR at that time.

Heading downstairs to eat, the chill, grey marble floors and walls presented an unappealing environment, made colder still by the huge echoing lobby, some 30 or 40 metres across, which was more suited to a railway concourse than executive hotel.

At that time Kiev wasn't the sort of place to wander around unaccompanied outside working hours, but the hotel's managers hadn't considered their guests' need for food or the opportunity to profit from their captive audience. It turned out this particular hotel boasted neither a restaurant, nor the option for room service. The grim receptionist directed me to the hotel's only nod to sustenance, the Black Cat Bar.

Like the rest of the hotel, it was vast and empty. I huddled in my chair at the bar, sipping an almost undrinkable coffee and wishing I'd thought to bring something to eat. One night without dinner wasn't going to kill me, but caffeine and an empty stomach promised a restless night ahead of a busy training programme.

Lost in my thoughts, I didn't notice an attractive blonde girl slip into the seat on my left or the more mature lady who settled in on my right until they started talking across me. It seemed odd given all the empty chairs and tables, but what the heck.

In the dingy low light of the bar it was hard to get a proper look at the women. The blonde was very young, probably too young, but it was always difficult to tell whether the women of Slavic origin were 13 or 30. Fortunately I never felt any desire to pay for company, although I was all too aware of the high value these women placed on connecting with a westerner. The older woman, a brunette whose unlikely hair made her look like a drag queen, was not visually rewarding. As she moved closer, I was aware of her pock-marked skin and the sour taint of her breath.

It transpired my older companion spoke English and we chatted for 20 minutes or so before I made my excuses and left them to their conversation.

The following evening, I returned to the hotel with a small group of trainees who were attending the course from the Crimea. It being too great a distance to travel each day for the course, they too were 'lucky' enough to be staying at the hotel, and we set out across the tundra of the lobby, heading for the distant reception to check them all in.

Crossing the concourse, I was spotted by the more mature of my companions from the Black Cat Bar, who assailed me to chat some more. It was an innocuous conversation until she announced loudly that her friend really liked me, and had been keen to have sex…

Standing surrounded by trainees and colleagues, I waited for the ground to open and swallow me whole, but no. Embarrassment wasn't done with me yet.

"It was not possible to go with you because she has a problem 'down there.'"

The lady, concerned I should understand her limited language skills, rubbed her nether regions furiously to get her message across.

I'm not sure which was more inflamed, her groin or my blood pressure.

Mortified, embarrassed, and totally out of control of the situation, I shepherded my astonished trainees at speed to the check in desk and ensured one of them was always nearby for the duration of my stay in Kiev.

Chapter Thirty-Eight :

Leaving Minsk

Towards the end of my time in Russia I was sent to Belarus to run a course in the city of Minsk.

Rostislav and his cousin had joined me for the second part of the course. They were concerned about the lack of respect I had received in Kiev, and wanted to lay down the law with managers in Minsk to prevent a repeat. No one would put a foot wrong while the two men were there, and the training ran without incident.

We were scheduled to return to Moscow early on Saturday morning. On arrival at Minsk airport there was no listing for our flight – the departure boards didn't even mention it. Enquiring at the desk we were informed no planes were flying to Moscow that day...

"You are at the wrong airport" said the disinterested woman in charge of information. It transpired we were at Minsk 1 airport and should have been at the unimaginatively titled Minsk 2, some 40km outside the city. But we would be too late anyway, she told us, the check in would be closed.

We dashed to the taxi rank and Rostislav threw $100 dollars at a driver who drove maniacally along the tree lined road to Minsk 2 with zero regard for anyone else on the road. The dollars provided the motivation to exceed all speed limits in a car which wasn't designed for rally driving, let alone the Grand Prix speeds he achieved.

Fortunately, the road was relatively clear, and we arrived at the airport and ran to the departure lounge on the first floor. We could see the runway and our plane taxiing towards it, waiting to take off.

Rostislav and his cousin handed out $100 bills to everyone in a uniform, promising more if they could get to get the flight to wait for us. Thousands of dollars changed hands and it worked. The plane pulled off the taxiway, and negotiations completed, the three of us stood in a triangle whilst the immigration officers, baggage checks and passport officer worked around us.

Legalities complete, we were driven in an airport car out to the spot where the plane had stopped. Climbing up the hastily acquired steps (another $100 for the handler), we walked onto the plane with the rest of the occupants craning their necks to see if they recognised these men who could stop a plane from taking off.

The Belavia plane was a twin turbo prop, ancient and probably bought second hand from Aeroflot, the Russian national airline. Neither carrier was known for high levels of safety or comfort.

The pilots and senior crew rewarded for their patience, the door was closed and we took off bound for Moscow, only to be caught in an incredible storm. It hit the fragile plane just half an hour out from Minsk. At this time flying in Russia was known to be dangerous; you took your life in your hands, and after a while it was easy to get blasé about the risks. On this occasion, even well-travelled Rostislav and his cousin were shaking with fear, their knuckles white as they gripped the wobbling seats in front of them. I figured if they were scared, then maybe I should be too.

Eventually, somewhat bruised and thinking perhaps going to the wrong airport in the first place had been divine intervention, we landed safely in Moscow. As we descended the steps, I tried not to notice the duct tape holding the plane together and vowed never to fly Belavia again....

Of all the rough flights I had in my career, that was, beyond a doubt, the one where I expected to meet my maker.

Chapter Thirty-Nine :

Lithuania to Latvia

Joachim married Katya and relocated to the Philip Morris cigarette manufacturing plant in Klaipėda, Lithuania. By this time, I'd decided to leave Moscow, as working for Rosinter and the long periods of time away from Leila had rather lost its shine. As Joachim needed some extra help, I agreed to do some lucrative consultancy work for his company.

Philip Morris was very dominant in the region and used every angle to obtain positive publicity to encourage use of their cigarette brand, including sponsorship of major cultural events. As I was preparing to take my leave on a Friday afternoon, Joachim and I were asked to represent the company at an important orchestral concert sponsored by the company which happened to be taking place that night in Riga, the capital of neighboring Latvia. It was no problem to change my flights and the company would put us up in an excellent hotel in Riga.

As ever with these things, no one senior wanted to go, but the sponsor was expected to attend to schmooze the great and the good of Riga. No one really talked about the risks of smoking back then, so neither Joachim nor I had any qualms about the jaunt. It sounded like a great wheeze and a fun way to spend a weekend.

Riga is around three hours due north of Klaipėda and spinning past Joachim's place to pick up a surprised Katya, we hit the road.

It sounds like the beginning of a bad joke… "an Englishman, a German and a Russian go to a concert" …

The challenges started with Lithuania being on western time and Latvia on eastern-European time… we would instantly lose an hour the moment we crossed the border – but it was travelling between the two countries which almost scuppered the trip. Joachim and I with our European passports waltzed through unimpeded – not Katya. She was taken to one side and interrogated for what seemed like hours, her papers checked, phone calls made, senior security officers involved and us standing waiting becoming more frustrated by the minute, but unable to do or say anything to hasten the process.

Russians weren't welcome in Latvia, and Katya had better have a darn good reason for going there.

With the time ticking by and no end in sight for the cross-examination, we were on the verge of abandoning the visit and returning to Lithuania. Government bureaucracy was all set to win against the corporate power of Philip Morris. In other places we might have handed out bribes in the form of packets of fags, but not here....

At the last possible minute, Katya was released, and we threw ourselves into the car and on to Riga.

Of course, we were late for the concert. I seemed to make a habit of tardy arrivals and last-minute tyre-screeching halts outside theatres and other elegant venues. The concert had already started, and as the evening-dress-clad highest echelons of Latvian society, along with a few politicians and their guests, were listening appreciatively in the auditorium, we stayed outside rather than create a scene.

The interval was awash with meet and greet. Joachim and Katya pressed the flesh with me, pretending to be Philip Morris executives with a keen interest in the artistic endeavors of Latvia. You can get away with a lot by pretending not to understand what people are saying!

Goodness knows what promises we made that night, but we made the most of the opportunity to see Riga before an uneventful return to Lithuania.

Chapter Forty :

Time runs away

Moving to Hatfield Garden Village was more than a change of location for Leila. A long-time smoker with a 20-a-day habit and zero interest in exercise, she decided to give up cigarettes and cut back on her drinking to improve her health. "The Finns", she told me, "have a famously addictive personality. They also have determination and the will to succeed".

Leila's Nordic upbringing made her very exacting in the ways she liked to do things. This was as relevant to peeling carrots and stirring gravy as it was to more intimate aspects of our life. She came from a family who spent hours hunched over a hole in a frozen lake ice fishing for parts of the year, even when the fish weren't biting, and the willpower to focus on the job in hand translated into all aspects of Leila's life.

She would take on a new challenge and never half-heartedly. Whatever she did Leila would throw herself into it, body and soul.

At one point she decided to train in massage, and as with everything else, she had to do it properly. Leila spent endless hours studying anatomy and physiology, along with the various techniques and traditions associated with the practice. She became an exceptionally good masseuse, all whilst working full time at the building society. She invested a lot of money and an incredible amount of time and adapted the spare room into a welcoming treatment space.

Ultimately though, once her determination had seen her through to graduation and she became qualified, Leila had no interest in marketing her new talent and moved onto the next passion.

From my perspective I was more impulsive. Yes, I could focus on running my training courses and our burgeoning property business, but whilst I was driven and diligent workwise, it didn't overtake my life in the way Leila's projects could. We were similar in many ways, but expected and received different outcomes.

Leila's first jog around the block nearly killed her but she'd made a decision, and there was no way she was giving up. Gradually she improved her distance, speed, and lung power. As her confidence increased, she joined the Welwyn Garden City Runners and began training with a group rather than on her own. Within a year or so she had conquered 5k, 10k and half marathons. When the opportunity arose, she would travel with the team to events around the UK and return with yet another medal around her neck.

Leila Paris Marathon

Meanwhile, I was working on being a step-parent, a role I fell into quite easily. I always felt I'd be a good father, although the opportunity had never arisen. Initially, although we talked of increasing our family, Leila's experience of pregnancy and Sarah's birth had been difficult, so she wasn't in any hurry to try childbirth again. In any case, being pregnant wouldn't fit into Leila's fitness regime. Years later we both regretted our decision, but by that time it was too late.

Instead, I enjoyed life in our new home which backed onto the old aerodrome at Hatfield. This was a popular filming location for blockbuster features, and I could sit in the garden and watch epics like Saving Private Ryan and Band of Brothers being filmed to an accompaniment of booms, bangs and enemy aircraft activity.

Leila was a mortgage advisor for the Abbey National Building Society which was later absorbed into banking giant Santander. I was beginning to do more international work across Europe, but still spent a lot of time training staff in the UK.

Thinking ahead towards our long-term future, we made a decision to buy more rental properties to supplement our company pensions, the plan being to build a portfolio of properties. One year later, property prices slumped, and our little rental empire was worth considerably less than we'd paid for it while the mortgage interest rate hit 15%.

This was crippling, even with two decent incomes and like many others at the time, we wondered if the property market would ever recover. After some shrugging and soul searching, we decided we were in it for the long haul and stayed with it – the best decision we could have made – and this was the beginning of our small but lucrative property portfolio.

In the meantime, Leila's wanderlust was being thwarted by our regular visits to my apartment in Calpe, so we sold the Spanish apartment to ease her boredom and started vacationing around the globe.

In many ways our destinations were dictated by Leila's passion for marathon running. Having made the step up from half to full marathons, she would run the race and we would take time out for a holiday afterwards. From Hawaii to Paris and many places in between we saw the world via the marathon circuit. Leila was planning one event after another, and our holiday schedule was booked well in advance. A little like Forrest Gump, she just kept running.

Leila Jersey Marathon

The move to Rosinter and working full time in Moscow had meant I was away for six weeks at a stretch rather than being home every weekend. Although travelling for work had escalated during our relationship, this was a new level. Leila was quite relaxed about the time apart; she had her running and a wide circle of friends and loved the independence of life without having to factor me coming and going each weekend.

I wasn't blind to the fact that her chosen running companions were men. Firstly Dave, and then Denys were constantly on hand to encourage her.

Suave, super-fit Denys was a Frenchman who had relocated to England to work as a translator for a multi-national company. His tall, dark Mediterranean good looks meant he attracted a lot of female attention. Recently divorced, he had a girlfriend who lived elsewhere but spent quite a lot of time with him.

Denys was the kind of guy who thought nothing of running three marathons over the course of a weekend or completing ten in ten days. Yes, he was that man! An international sporting champion, who seldom heard the word "Non" whispered by female lips.

He was a committed vegan long before it was fashionable, so eating out with Denys was a nightmare. Visiting marathon locations around the world with him and the other team runners meant we often ate together. Inevitably Denys, being the one with the 'special dietary requirements' always chose a pizzeria in the belief he would receive a meal devoid of animal products. This was the 1990s! All I can say is it's a good job he wasn't living in Russia! Everything on the menu contained something Denys couldn't eat and if we hadn't been too polite to abandon him, we'd have gone elsewhere for steak and chips cooked in lashings of lard followed by rich dairy ice cream!

The Welwyn Garden City runners were part of our social life as much as the friends we'd made at our favourite watering hole. Whenever I was in the country, Friday night was spent at the John Bunyan in Wheathampsted. If Leila was home, she would come with me, but often she was away with the team, preparing to run one marathon or another around the UK.

After leaving Rosinter I focused on managing our property portfolio and taking on short term contracts which kept me closer to home. My reputation in the business world meant I was sought out for behavioural, motivational, and team building projects, and this was both financially beneficial and an enjoyable way to spend my time.

A happy man

Being back in the UK also meant I was able to travel with Leila for the international running events. I tended to avoid the national ones. There was little attraction in spending a weekend with a race team when you weren't taking part. There was too much standing around, and when you've seen one budget city centre hotel, you've seen them all. Leila would room share with other team members and reminiscent of my experience with amateur dramatics, what happened on tour, stayed on tour.

Dave and Denys made no secret of their closeness to Leila and often seemed to forget I was in the picture. On a marathon trip to Phoenix, Arizona, I sat across the breakfast table from Leila whilst Dave and Denys sparred over her like rutting stags, each convinced she was theirs.

It was hard to take exception to the presence of other men in Leila's life. When I was away, out of range of regular contact or conversation for weeks at a time (these were the days before the internet and mobile phone calls), it was obvious she wasn't going to sit around at home. She was a gregarious, lively, and entertaining companion.

I found it a stretch to be with one person, and I too had flirtations and dalliances which provided a distraction from thinking about where, or with whom, Leila might be spending her free time.

We never asked one another, and neither of us chose to tell.

When we were in the same place at the same time, we were devoted to one another. That's all there was to it.

Leila celebrates her 100th marathon

Chapter Forty-One :

A Deeper Connection

Back home in the UK, with only short trips away for consultancy work and time to relax, our time and connection became even more precious.

The lifestyle Leila and I led together was unlike that of any of our friends or family. We had learned to be independent of one another for my work and her hobbies, and we certainly each had personal attachments from time to time which we chose not to share with one another, although we both implicitly knew.

Even once I moved back to the UK full time, my days were often occupied with running the rental properties, doing my consultancy work, and spending time at the gym.

In any other couple this could have been fatal to the relationship, but for Leila and me, the connection ran much more deeply. We thrived on our unique arrangement, and the occasional infidelity had no real relevance to either of us.

The one thing which stood out was our ability to communicate. Each night as we sat down to supper, on her days off and our holidays we would talk about anything and everything.

We loved to walk together, escaping on a Tuesday to the beach at Hunstanton in Norfolk or, if we could get away, an expedition to the West Country, taking stages of the Southwest Coastal Path until it was almost complete. On these walks we would talk endlessly, filling these excursions with laughter and tears, creating memories, and strengthening the profound bond between us.

It's hard to describe the depth of feeling we shared, especially as I may come across as cavalier or selfish in terms of the women in my life. With Leila it was all and everything, transcending the mundane and tapping into something I've never known anyone else experience as we did.

It wasn't always glorious for me however, as my sporting prowess was usually left in Leila's wake! When we first went to a ski resort, Leila took to downhill skiing immediately. She had a head start from her native Finland, having skied to and from school during the deep snow of frigid Finnish winters and was adept as a trail and cross-country skier. She took to the much steeper alpine conditions easily and perhaps it was the genetic pre-disposition which meant Sarah also thrived in the snow.

As a family Leila, Sarah, and her husband Lee, along with Lee's parents were all excellent skiers. Even the grandchildren took to it quickly, racing around like tiny, fearless, bundled up ducklings, quickly graduating from ski school to the slopes.

I, on the other hand, loathed the annual ski trip. I never became an accomplished skier, nor could I see the pleasure in strapping two planks to uncomfortable boots and throwing yourself off a mountain. It just didn't do it for me, although I recognise it is a tremendous buzz for many enthusiasts.

Now I look back with the eyes of time and experience, I understand my alpha male status was compromised by this sport in which I had zero skill and even less inclination to take part. I'd never have admitted to that however, not even to Leila.

Instead after several trips to various resorts across Europe I announced to Leila that in future I was perfectly happy for everyone to go without me. I'd stay home and look after the cat.

As any non-skiing companion will know, the days can be long and empty while everyone else is on the piste. By this time, I'd gone way beyond wasting hours on private instructors yelling at me to snow plough or bend my knees. I hate the cold, have no desire to challenge the elements and I'm gregarious. That's me!

Wherever I am in the world, I like to chat about anything and everything in a warm, convivial atmosphere and if I'm on holiday my chosen attire is shorts and a T-shirt. In contrast, the whole focus of time in an alpine village, regardless of the country or age of the participants, is to ski, talk about the runs, endlessly discuss snow quality and lifts before planning the next day's routes, all while eating heavy food and drinking to excess before going to bed early to get a head start on the next day's 'fun'. Short of the occasional spa, there usually isn't much to do for the disinterested mate whilst everyone else is off seeking snow-related adventure.

Snow Queen Leila

      To the disappointment of both me and the cat, Leila wasn't having any of it, and refused to even consider going without me. This was an example of the strength of our partnership in relation to the family, and the value of spending quality time together.

Whilst working apart for weeks at a time was routine, being together for holidays was non-negotiable. I packed my thermals and went on what, as it transpired, was Leila's last glacial spree.

Chapter Forty-Two :

Vision

By 2002 I was still doing occasional consultancy assignments, mainly as a paid hobby. I was always fascinated by the new opportunities for adventure and was headhunted into various projects without ever having to apply for a role.

My former colleague Trevor, who jumped ship with me from Kodak, knew my reputation for providing innovative training and development across many countries and disparate organizations. He asked if I would take on a project for a well-respected people development organization – Vision.

The main location was in the woods within Wokefield Park, Basingstoke, a hotel and golf complex. As well as having a training facility which looked like a large scout hut, it also had a low-ropes and high-ropes course set up in the grounds.

My initial development training sessions were primarily in the training room and occasionally on the low ropes course. It wasn't particularly lucrative, but that didn't really matter. I enjoyed the work and collaborating with inspiring fellow providers. They always say you are the product of the five people you spend the most time with, and they were a great bunch of people.

You would think the low ropes course was pretty safe, but even being just a metre above the ground proved damaging to one participant. With no local ambulance available, a rescue helicopter was dispatched, causing a sensation at the hotel and a frisson of excitement amongst the golfers. With everyone assuming there had been a catastrophic accident on the high ropes, the news of a trainee with a damaged ankle was something of an anticlimax.

After working with the team for a while, I was invited to train and qualify as a high ropes instructor. The advantage to Vision was that I became an even more useful asset to their programme.

Although I was deeply uncomfortable with heights, I'm always open to new experiences so naturally I said 'Yes'.

The high ropes are the kind of equipment you see in adventure parks. As you can imagine, the safety requirements are extreme, as a fall from such a height can have a life changing or even fatal outcome.

Training was intense, very physical with a lot of technical content. Most of the trainees were in their 20s, young and extremely fit. We initially practiced on the low ropes course - not too far to fall! Part of this was learning how to 'rescue at height,' an exercise where one person rescues another from the top of a pole in an emergency situation.

The technique is for the rescuer to climb to the top of the pole and attach themselves to the 'casualty' belt-to-belt. Then, once secure, they would cut the casualty's safety rope and lower them gently to the ground using the rescuer's rope to support them both.

Sounds simple doesn't it? Actually, it's massively harder than it sounds. We frequently got so tangled that, much to their amusement, the ground crew had to unpick us from a spaghetti of ropes!

Eventually we felt confident to practice real rescues at the maximum height of 18 metres. Always aware of the risks, together with the need to use kit sustainably, the 'victim' was attached to an older rope and the 'rescuer' given a spanking new rope in a different colour. Knowing one from the other was vital as just before the descent one of the ropes would have to be cut.

If I was on a red and blue rope and my supposedly unconscious companion was on a green and yellow, you'd hear them muttering "green and yellow, green and yellow" as I wielded my scissors to save us both from certain doom. You might think as a climber I'd have a trusty knife to do the deed, but as we'd learned, knives were a risky strategy. The force needed for one slice of a knife could take out both ropes with one slash. Kitchen scissors might have been less macho, but they were a whole lot safer!

Training on the high ropes meant I was rescued as often as necessary to support the training of other team members. On one occasion a young female casualty inadvertently moved into a position which meant she descended awkwardly on our shared rope whilst sitting on my face. With three sets of burning cheeks, it was a great relief to reach the ground. Fortunately, this was before cameras on mobile phones, because the ground crew were still laughing hours later.

I'd become comfortable climbing and had learned to trust the kit and my ability. When the final assessment day came, it went really well until the instructor asked us to complete our knot tying demonstrations behind our backs. Logically, he explained, it was highly likely we would have to tie knots in unusual situations. It was a perfectly sound idea, but something none of us had done before. After much grumbling we all managed to do a fair job of it – with the added bonus of being able to untie our hands from behind our backs if things ever got sticky!

Ultimately, I passed my high ropes training qualification aged 60, the oldest participant by about 30 years.

Learning something new and trusting in your ability to do it in any situation applies to numerous things in all our lives. And regardless of what they say, you can teach an old dog new tricks.

So I thought I'd extend my knowledge by trying yet another hobby. I'd always loved the idea of sailing, although never did as much as I would have liked on the Kodak boat. With a thought to do more with this hobby, Sarah's husband, his best man Dave and I signed up for a 'Competent Crew' course on the Solent just off the Isle of Wight.

We were out on a cold, wet day in rough seas doing a man-overboard training session. To be honest, we probably shouldn't have even left the dock but the skipper, a man more used to training Royal Marine commandos at the Lympstone Naval base, wasn't about to make any concessions for us.

Someone spotted a kite surfer in the water clinging to his board. His canopy had come down around him with the lengths of white cords wrapping around his arms and legs. The guy was in serious trouble and our rescue training took on a very grim new dimension.

The skipper carefully steered as close as he dared, recognizing we had only one chance to raise the man out of the water before the propeller became entangled in the lines of the kite. Following the skipper's instructions to work in coordination, it was imperative to pull the surfer and his kit onto the yacht in one go or risk scuppering our own vessel and finding ourselves the subject of an RNLI rescue, which would have been very embarrassing for our tutor.

To everyone's relief, we got the bedraggled man on board and radioed the Coast Guard to confirm his safety and our intention to land him at a beach nearby. The Coast Guard, with typical cool in the face of adversity, told us they already knew - they had been watching us throughout.

Chapter Forty-Three :

The New Mrs. Higgs

By the time Leila and I had been together 25 years it felt as though we should make it permanent. Sarah had grown up and left home then married Lee and moved some distance from our home. Despite that, they were regular guests on any Sunday when Leila wasn't running. Her roast dinner would always draw a crowd.

With Sarah living in a home of her own, and a mother in her own right to a handsome little lad called Harvey, it was just the two of us and I wasn't getting any younger. Being aware of my years, I wanted to make sure Leila was protected should anything happen to me. Aside from anything else, spending time in Russia and knowing of people who met with unexpected 'accidents' or simply disappeared, had me focused on my own mortality.

I asked my lovely Leila to marry me and in August 2010 she became my wife.

A quick registry office wedding was followed by a beautiful reception with our families at Sopwell House in St Albans.

Wedding Day

It really felt, after all those years together, like the right thing to do. Leila had been less inclined to tie the knot after her earlier failed marriage, but she understood, aside from the practicalities of an inheritance (after all I was significantly older than she was), that this was important to me. Once we were married, she was comfortable with being my wife, and happy to have succumbed to my charms at last – with one exception – she refused to be known as 'Mrs. Higgs'.

Whenever we stayed in a hotel, Leila would insist on having time to dress for dinner. I would smarten up and take myself off to the bar for a G&T or rich merlot to give her space. At the appointed hour she would appear at the door and sashay into my arms. Every man in the place would turn to see this vision, thinking this was his night, but she only had eyes for me. I was the luckiest man alive.

Now working abroad was over, it wasn't exotic or high maintenance, it was simply love.

My beautiful wife

I was happy, and Leila was the centre of my life. There was no question of anyone else in my thoughts, and although she was still running and Denys was her training partner, we had settled into a wonderful phase in our marriage.

Chapter Forty-Four :

Stopped In Our Tracks

Fate sometimes has a way of kicking dust in your face. Away for a marathon in Krakow, Poland, Denys had commented that Leila was always doubled up in pain at the end of a race. She'd evidently brushed his concerns away for quite some time until finally she made an appointment to see the GP. Had she taken notice, things may have been very different.

Over several visits the doctor prescribed various medications, eventually reaching the conclusion Leila had a stomach ulcer. A biopsy was necessary, but perfectly straightforward to confirm the diagnosis, so nothing to worry about.

All my underlying concerns about being considerably older than Leila, and her being left alone if something happened to me, paled to insignificance when my beautiful girl was diagnosed with stomach cancer just a year after our wedding.

Her chemotherapy started soon afterwards but was accompanied by side effects so bad she had to be admitted to hospital full time whilst she awaited surgery. In the run up to Christmas 2011 she was alone in a side room on a busy ward. Desperate for help, her call-bell was left unanswered while Leila writhed in crippling pain.

When a nurse finally took notice there was no option other than to transfer her under blue light to the Lister hospital. Even there, the medical team's expertise was inadequate to manage Leila's condition. She was again transferred, this time to the specialist cancer centre at Mount Vernon. From being perilously close to death prior to surgery, she fought back with incredible perseverance and speed to what appeared to be a good recovery.

As the year progressed, her health fluctuated wildly. During the autumn we were told the cancer had spread and she became very ill again. We knew now the outcome was inevitable. The pain she endured was unbearable and for the second Christmas Leila was in agony and everyone who loved her had to witness the trauma she was experiencing. Even now I can't bear Christmas, those memories have tarnished my thoughts to such a degree.

In early 2013 there was no question Leila needed palliative care to keep her comfortable for the last part of her life. The time in the hospice made her more comfortable, but we knew we didn't have long.

That last Valentine's Day was bittersweet. Visiting the hospice with a heavily pregnant Sarah, Leila was surprised to receive two valentine's cards, one from me and one from Harvey, who was just 3 years old. She was overjoyed. They meant the world to her.

Leila, as ever wanting to be her lovely self, apologized for not getting me a card. I didn't need cards, I just wanted my girl healthy, happy and at home with me again.

She died the next evening, knowing she would never see her second grandchild fill our home with joy.

Ilona arrived six weeks later. She grew into a vivacious little sprite, the image of her mother and grandmother and as determined and outspoken as the pair of them combined.

After Leila's death her remaining relatives travelled to the UK for the cremation. This is traditionally a reflective and very formal event in Finnish culture and each member of the family had to touch the coffin as part of the ritual which follows a parting.

Shortly afterwards Sarah and I flew to Finland with the ashes in accordance with Leila's wish to be interred in the family grave. We stayed with her sister Kykkä in Helsinki and on the day of the burial she drove us several hours north to Lemi close to the Russian border where we met up with the rest of the family. It was a day of drama, overwhelming sadness and finding a way to celebrate a life well lived.

In my grief I hadn't considered the necessity for reams of paperwork to complete in Finnish and have witnessed before the ceremony could take place in the Lutheran church of her childhood. The graveyard was foreboding, at least it felt so to me.

In March there is hardly any daylight so far north and the dark, granite monuments and obelisks looked like something from a horror movie. Most were engraved with complex, heavily accented Finnish names while the one prepared for my girl in this distant, such isolated part of the globe bore the unexpected English name Leila Higgs.

Eventually, legalities concluded, I knelt and placed her ashes in the family plot. Leaving my beloved Leila to rest in the soil of her homeland, far from the life we had made together, I walked away a lost and hollow man, totally unprepared for life without her.

PART IV

A Change of Scene

Chapter Forty-Five :

The Creeping Darkness

Within a year of Leila's death, and still in the depths of paralyzing grief, I was dealing with my own medical crisis.

A slightly swollen and tender area close to my left ear was giving me increasing cause for concern. The first time I visited my local GP, I was fobbed off. At the second visit, a month later, his opinion was that although there was a red, angry lesion at the back of my jaw, there was nothing really wrong. His suggestion was that perhaps next time I saw a dentist I could "mention it to them".

I made an appointment immediately, and the dentist referred me directly to hospital. This was serious.

A diagnosis of stage 4 retro-dental carcinoma led to a season ticket for the Mount Vernon Cancer Centre, one of the top specialist hospitals in the UK.

The original misdiagnosis by my GP had resulted in a dangerous delay in expert clinical intervention. His comment afterwards that he had only seen a couple of cases in his 30-year career, and that these had been in heavy smokers, did nothing to reassure me about the missed opportunity for an earlier referral to a specialist.

My consultant's treatment plan was for me to undergo a few sessions of chemotherapy followed by six weeks of targeted radiotherapy. It was made clear this was my only option for a long-term solution. With less than a 40% chance of survival, I had to stay the course.

I was warned the treatment would be challenging but there was nothing else to be done. I was fitted for a special mask which would bolt my head to the table and along with straps pinning the rest of my body down, I would be unable to move. I was Frankenstein's monster, longing for my old life and wishing I was anywhere but here.

The radiation was targeted straight at the cancer cells and designed to be minimally invasive to the healthy areas of my head. Even in the brief time since Leila's diagnosis, cancer treatments had been enhanced. Medical research really is a wonderful thing, but this was to prove brutal.

At first, I didn't really feel anything. I drove myself in each day and trusted changes were happening for the better. Over the weeks the pain just grew. Four weeks in it was so intense I could no longer drive and had to rely on others to take me. I hated to be dependent, it just wasn't in my nature then, and nothing has changed even now.

It reached the point where I was sorely tempted to miss the appointments and take whatever outcome fate had in store for me, but the doctors spoke plainly. There was sound medical justification for sticking with it and completing the course because it was much more likely to be successful this way.

I'm not a quitter, and neither was Leila. This vile disease had beaten her, but hateful as it was, I needed to keep going for both of us.

The treatment made it impossible to eat, so each night I was hooked up to a drip for metered nutrition to be pumped into my chest. Fortunately, Milly, a slightly scatty, but deeply caring Anglo-Indian friend of Sarah stayed over each night to administer the treatment and monitor my condition. She wasn't local, living an hour's drive from Wheathampsted and working full-time, so it was a huge commitment for her. Most of the time I was out of it, lost in pain, fear, and grief. Milly's calm presence kept me functioning as best I could. How she took care of me, did the drives night and morning, and worked full time I have no idea – that was the measure of the girl.

I desperately needed her support because I was barely able to function. Even after the treatment finished in June 2014, I was still taking all nutrition intravenously until the following September, experiencing significant and permanent weight loss of the worst kind. The physical and mental scars of that terrible time, combined with losing Leila, were deeply traumatic.

My heart felt raw, empty. Trying to deal with this whilst still in the depths of grief for Leila, giving up would have been an easy way out... but I knew she would want me to win, and I never wanted to go through this again.

After the last of the 30-day zapping appointments the technician congratulated me on making it through. It transpired most patients don't complete the course without a break. When the pain gets too much they just stop coming and only return when their condition deteriorates – and it's often too late.

My consultant warned me the treatment was so invasive the pain would continue to grow even after the radiation stopped, but after several weeks it would begin to subside. He was right, it was horrific, and I wouldn't wish this on anyone.

Dealing with the physical and mental trauma of this time whilst my body and mind tried to rebuild itself was lonelier and more desolate than I can write. I was living comfortably, rattling about even, in our large house in a sought-after village in Hertfordshire. To an outside observer my life looked easy. I had it made. No worries about money, holidays in the UK and abroad, but really, I was running away...

I was running from the grey life, the desolation and just bumbling through. Something had to change.

Chapter Forty-Six :

Graham

During my recovery from cancer, I had little interest or energy to keep an eye on the property portfolio Leila and I had built up. I needed an extra pair of hands; someone I could trust to check and maintain the buildings while I regained my strength.

My family had become distant, but perhaps I was distant from them. They were wrapped in their own lives, and we didn't have much in common. There wasn't anyone I could share the responsibility for managing the properties with, and I wasn't ready to sell up, so I placed an advertisement with the intention of recruiting someone. They would require handyman skills and could be relied on to act in my best interests.

Enter Graham. He was in his mid-50s, a strong, well-built man who had spent his career in construction before emigrating to Spain and subsequently returning to the UK after just a couple of years abroad.

He was good company, and I felt immediately at ease with him. We became firm friends in addition to his maintaining the properties. He's now my right-hand man and someone I can trust to give wise and sensible information in relation to property. We may not always agree wholeheartedly, but he can be relied on to have a balanced discussion in order to assess both sides of a situation.

The great thing about Graham was his ability to be ahead of the game. He has excellent contacts with local trades, and within an hour of a tenant reporting a problem, Graham would be on it, solve it or find someone who could, and the status quo would be regained. Having that degree of support took a load off my shoulders, I didn't feel so alone anymore, and started to enjoy being a 'property baron'. I was even considering buying some more buy-to-let homes.

Graham, along with his slight and energetic partner Maureen, urged me to be more active and we became a good team. They could see I was living a grey life in the doldrums and encouraged me to think about my lifestyle in a more positive way. The future could be brighter if I wanted it to be.

With Graham at my side, my time was freed up and I could begin travelling again. The combination of text, email and WhatsApp meant he could be in touch if the necessity arose, and I could trust him to always do a great job.

I was doing things people would have been jealous of, luxury holidays around the world and catching up with international friends who lived in exotic and not-so-exotic locations, but my heart wasn't in it. I travelled to escape Wheathampsted, but as soon as the return flight landed, the gloom descended again.

Chapter Forty-Seven :

Nathalie

My love of Spain, born years before when I had my place in the Costa Blanca, had led to a fair degree of street-Spanish. I could get by and even had some lessons, but I knew I could improve on my language skills, and in any case, I wanted to keep my brain learning new things.

I invested some time searching online for a Spanish teacher. I tried a couple of local options and had some lessons, but the teachers and I didn't quite gel.

I wasn't ready to give up, and a further search led to a bright, vivacious, outgoing French lady who also taught Spanish and Italian. We clicked from the very first lesson.

Nathalie made it fun. I began to look forward to our lessons in her modest apartment. I'm not sure where the laughter ended and the learning began, but my Spanish improved week by week.

Nathalie's clients were an extremely well-heeled bunch, and it's fair to say they enjoyed the high life which, as she certainly wasn't charging her worth, Nathalie heard about in their conversations, but never got to enjoy.

I felt the same. My family would tell me about visits to exclusive restaurants, but I wasn't invited to join them as I was probably not the best company back then. A passing comment led to my suggestion that Nathalie and I should have a fine-dining experience of our own.

It was the beginning of a deep and abiding friendship, not always balanced, and sometimes teetering on the brink of becoming more, especially on my part.

It was a relationship of sorts. I loved to take her out, she was sparkling company and our evenings at restaurants and tapas bars, where I ostensibly practiced my Spanish, grew into weekends away and then luxury holidays.

She was deliciously demanding, high maintenance, and I loved it. The light came back into my life, and I adored treating her with a little extravagance, just as I had with all the special women who had preceded her.

Our travels took us to Cuba, Spain, Malta and Dubai. We had a great time, always sleeping in separate rooms, and me giving Nathalie the space to explore these new destinations. We enjoyed Berber trips out into the desert, quad biking, boat trips and generally being tourists in places I would never have visited without her encouragement.

Nathalie's mother back in Bordeaux was sinking fast into dementia, and our holidays were meant to be an escape for her as much as a fun opportunity to spend time together, but the phone rang constantly, and she spent hours reassuring the elderly lady in rapid French rather than relaxing by the pool.

As much as Nathalie bought fun, her temper could be quick and volatile, especially after her mother's myriad concerns had bought her to the edge of reason.

Some of the rows we had were incendiary; I would shout, and she would scream, slam doors and I would reach the brink of finishing our arrangement. She was demanding, pouting, possessive and sometimes downright unreasonable, often blaming her 'European hot temper' and the need to "express my emotions because I am French" once she calmed down. From the outside a casual observer would have assumed we were married and on the verge of divorce.

The funny thing was, on the next day neither of us would remember what the row had been about, and we'd continue our holiday as though nothing had happened.

Nathalie would never admit to being a girlfriend, although we both thoroughly enjoyed the conversation, companionship, and the lifestyle we created for ourselves.

She encouraged me to bring my thinking up to the present. We'd shop and she gradually changed my style to a younger, more flattering look which suited me.

Nathalie's verve and zest for life was infectious. She brought me out of myself in ways which reminded me of the wild days before I'd settled with Leila, and Nathalie's fizzing energy eased the grief which had surrounded me for so long.

The relationship between us was delicately balanced. Whilst never intimate it was intense and tactile. We were deeply attached and had become powerfully important to one another despite the 25-year age gap. We spent a lot of time together, eating out, holidays, shopping, laughter, constant texts, and conversations. Indeed, it was everything you'd expect in a committed relationship. The problem was, we both wanted more. Love, romance, and sex were on our minds– just not with one another.

We were rebuilt emotionally through our friendship. I'd come to terms with my grief and was looking forward to my new life in Olney, whilst Nathalie had gained confidence along with an influx of new students for her language lessons and had started dancing at weekends. The dynamic between us was changing.

I think we knew it was coming, it was just a case of who blinked first. Even if we'd had an opportunity to meet a potential partner, we had left no space in our lives to nurture a relationship with someone new.

English is Nathalie's third, or perhaps fourth language, and the words she wanted to convey would have eluded her in such an emotional conversation face to face. Instead, she wrote the most beautiful 'Dear John' letter to explain why she felt it was time to put some distance between us.

I confess I was heartbroken at first. I'd feared the loss of my spirited companion and now it had happened, but as is often the case, the timing was perfect. My new life in Olney was beckoning and there wasn't a minute to lose.

Chapter Forty-Nine :

A New Beginning

Despite the memories of our time together, the home Leila and I had created, with her beautiful 'cooks' kitchen and the space which had once been filled with laughter, the house at Wheathampsted now felt cold and empty.

The house had become a dormitory and launch pad for numerous vacations. It was filled with ghosts, but they weren't keeping me close to Leila. These were spectres I'd created for myself, and they inhabited the tidy, soul-less place but ignored me. I know some widowed people can live on in a home they shared and derive a sense of connection with their beloved in the very fabric of the building. It wasn't that way for me. The chill was palpable, and I might as well have been one of my phantom housemates – I still felt dead inside.

Wheathampsted had lost its appeal, and I didn't socialize much. I thought perhaps downsizing somewhere different would give me the impetus to do more.

I had been spending a lot of time with Nathalie and, knowing of her intention to remain in her adopted hometown of Berkhamsted, I considered moving to be closer to her.

Deep down, I knew this wasn't the best idea I'd ever had, but getting away from the loneliness of Wheathampsted had become an obsession.

I believe most change happens in life when there is a combination of 'push' and 'pull'. The two were about to coincide.

Talking with my brother and mulling over my plans to relocate, he reminded me I'd always liked Olney, a honey-toned market town in Buckinghamshire. The market square and vibrant restaurant and coffee shop scene were attractive, and strangers said 'Hello'. It had a mellow community vibe about it and for the first time I actually considered that I could live somewhere new on my terms, and not simply because someone else lived there too.

Yes, my brother was nearby, perhaps three miles from the town. He'd be close enough but not on my doorstep and that would suit us both.

The summer weather was excellent that year. I spent a lot of time reconnoitering Olney and inevitably gravitated towards its traditional pubs and restaurants, along with many others from neighbouring villages. The high street was the ideal destination for a relaxed meal or catching up with friends. The residents of Olney were welcoming, with horse riders and dog owners greeting me on every walk, and even a walk along the high street would be peppered by conversations with strangers. I was drawn in to the genial, old-style small-town feeling, and knew this was where I wanted to be.

All that remained was to find the right house. It needed to be more compact and cosier than the cavernous space of the large renovated 1970s place I was leaving behind. I wanted a home in which I could bounce into the next part of my life, have guests to stay and enjoy the richness of country life and community… and perhaps I might meet someone to share it with – or at least invite friends round for an evening of warmth and congeniality.

Two or three days later, my brother and his wife Sandra saw a property for sale and immediately arranged a visit. Wasting no time, they called me up – "you have to see this place – NOW!"

And that was it, I'd found my home and made an offer. The house had barely touched the property market, but it was to be mine.

Selling the Wheathampstead house proved a bit of a slog. It had been on the market for quite a while and the agents organized viewings, but nothing came of them. It was as though the house was invisible - a ridiculous scenario in a highly sought after village.

Although the purchase of the Olney house was only in the early stages, I really needed Wheathampsted to sell in order to buy it outright. I could perhaps have liquidated other assets and waited it out, but I was ready to be free of the old house and my grey unhappy life.

Nathalie suggested I engaged Suzanne Roynon, an expert Interiors Therapist, to make the place feel more welcoming. Suzanne spent four hours with me, and the house came alive again. It sparkled with vibrant energy. Two days later it sold, and by the end of May, just four months after I viewed the new property, I had moved to Olney.

I was immediately invited to join local sports and social clubs. The brief chats I had enjoyed with locals turned into long relaxed lunches outside my nearest hostelry, 'The Cherry Tree' where I could watch the world go by.

After a couple of pints in the early evening when the traffic evaporated and the golden stone of the houses exuded mellow warmth long after the sun had gone down, I felt I was living the glorious lifestyle I'd experienced in rural France rather than being 10 minutes from the M1 in Buckinghamshire.

Reawakening my lost sociability after years of a lonely half-existence was exhilarating. I found myself with a contact list of new friends and an increasing network of interests. I reached the point where I had to schedule time for myself! Just a year before such a situation would have been unimaginable.

My hibernation was over – life had begun again.

Much as I enjoyed the walks and camaraderie, I still felt I had something to offer business. My years in the corporate world and decades of training gave me a store of useful knowledge and an accumulation of ready funds. I put feelers out for worthwhile opportunities to do something inspiring with my money. Interest rates were almost zero, so having a considerable sum sitting untouched in the bank wasn't much fun. I kept my ear to the ground and after discarding a couple of ideas which just didn't stack up, I became involved in a couple of local businesses as an Angel Investor.

Being in partnership in this way gave me an intention to see the companies succeed without having my nose to the grindstone or any real responsibility. I could take a detached view, offer advice if requested, and a gentle nudge if it wasn't. My time was my own and I was back in the game.

I knew I'd made the right decision to move to Olney, and as time went on I made many new friends who became a supportive and fun coterie for meals out and visits to the local pub I'd invested in. My home was always open for visitors and overnight guests.

And then the Covid 19 Pandemic hit.

Like almost everyone, the covid lockdowns hit my social life hard. Living alone I had become emotionally reliant on the connections I'd made, the excellent food available at the many restaurants in Olney and having a group of friends on the doorstep. Suddenly my safety net had vanished. It just wasn't the same seeing people at a distance or online, and although I'm reasonably adept in the kitchen, cooking for one didn't feed my soul. I missed my friends.

It gave me a lot of time to think. The house was perfectly adequate for a fit and healthy version of me, but what would happen if I needed nursing care at some point in the future?

I met Claire, a very smart, diminutive blonde with long, wavy Hollywood hair and sparkling eyes soon after I moved to Olney. She's immensely sociable, chats to everyone in the local pubs and seems to know most of the townspeople well. At first glance you'd never imagine she's an astute and highly successful businesswoman, but first impressions can be deceptive.

Aside from being a single mum to two of the nicest kids I know, Claire is generous to a fault with all her friends. She owns and manages a local elderly care home with such compassion for her patients, it warms the heart. The administration of the staff, endless Government rules and regulations and of course her 22 residents is staggering, not to mention the physical aspects of taking on shifts where necessary.

We stayed in touch through the pandemic and despite the extraordinary pressure Claire was under, she was always the first person to offer help when she thought I needed it. Claire became a treasured addition to my life, thinking ahead and encouraging me to enjoy my golden years to the full.

She knew something about my circumstances and said without hesitation that if I could make space for a live in carer should the need arise, then I would be better off both financially and practically by remaining in my own home.

That wouldn't be possible in the relatively small home I was living in, and her words started the process of another move.

Chapter Fifty :

A Forever Home

Ironically, having downsized from the cavernous 1970s place in Wheathampstead, I now wanted to upgrade to a place which would give ample room for a live in carer and be a comfortable home for me until that became necessary.

I wouldn't be sorry to leave my home with its beautiful courtyard garden. It had served a purpose and given me an entry point to Olney. Now it was time to find my 'forever home'.

I started viewing larger properties in the town and villages nearby, but none were quite what I was looking for. Finding my way to a couple of new estates being built in the town was illuminating. I hadn't considered a new build, but when I sat down and talked with Interiors Therapist Suzanne Roynon, she encouraged me to make a list of all of the elements important to include in a new home.

Ultimately, armed with a record of the 'essentials,' 'bonuses' and 'non-negotiables' for an ideal home, I found a new build with a specification which felt right. I like to think I'm open to new things, although perhaps with the science being over 5000 years old, Feng Shui can't be described as 'new'. However, this was the first time I'd ever used it to decide which of the four properties available, within the specification and design I had chosen, would be the most auspicious for me.

After a day checking compass directions, build dates and the topography of the land, we identified two properties which would be described as 'luckier' than the others. It was interesting to see the process of elimination which incorporated useful elements I hadn't considered; like the flow of people past a couple of the properties to go to the recreation area and the location of the third close to an intersection. Ultimately one property stood out and that was the one I chose.

During the warmest July on record to that date, I moved in and my latest 'new life' began. But that's another story!

Conclusion

Looking back over my autobiography, I've had excitement, lucky breaks, met amazing people, loved well, and been loved. Along the way I've struggled, been close to meeting my maker more than once, experienced heartache and grief beyond measure. Above all, I've survived.

But if you know me, and I hope you do by now, you'll know simply being a survivor was never going to be enough.

If you take anything away from this book, please regard every day as a chance to be who you want to be, to achieve and accomplish, play to your strengths, and enjoy the journey.

Regardless of your background, you choose to stand tall or be walked over. Choice is a powerful thing and it's the only thing entirely in your hands.

I'm sitting in the reading nook of my delightful new residence, looking out across the fields, and indulging in a little breathing space before my next big adventure begins.

Living in a house which nurtures and supports me at the deepest level and feels welcoming the moment I walk through the door means I'm truly 'home'. I've found an anchor which has been missing since Leila's untimely death.

The year since I relocated has given me a new lease of life, renewing my enthusiasm, and opening my eyes to the opportunities waiting for me. At an age when most people might be comfortably retired, I'm motivated to transform 80 years of experience into fresh business ventures, travel to places I've never been and enjoy these years to the full.

With Joachim - surprise guest at my 80th birthday party

I'm blessed with supportive friends, a brother and sister-in-law who have my back and to be part of a community in which I'm appreciated. I'm happy when I once believed happiness had gone forever.

I'm choosing to swagger into the ninth decade of my life and enjoy the ride. I think that's the best way to be!

Michael Higgs
November 2023

Acknowledgements

My gratitude and thanks to Graham Barnes, Adele-Marie Hartshorn and everyone who encouraged me to write this book.

To Claire and Lucy whose enthusiasm and prompting was a constant motivation.

To Suzanne Roynon whose patience and inspiration transformed my homes, and whose attention to detail kept me on track to complete this book.

And especially to Nathalie, whose vivacity lit my way out of the darkness and invited delight, fun and new connections, while reigniting my joy in travelling the world.

These people, whom I value as treasured friends, transformed my existence and brought my words, which would otherwise have remained fireside stories and anecdotes, into this book. This is the story of my life so far…

About the Author

Michael Higgs is an entrepreneur and mentor based in Buckinghamshire. He recently entered his ninth decade and is living his best life on his own terms. His passion for travel, friendship, conversation, and great company are undiminished.

Printed in Great Britain
by Amazon

48410941R00155